Iphis and Iante

A Play Based on
Ovid's *Metamorphoses*

ISAAC DE BENSERADE

Iphis and Iante

A Play Based on
Ovid's *Metamorphoses*

Edited by

Marianne Legault

Translated by

Ramine Adl

The Modern Language Association of America
New York 2025

85 Broad Street, New York, New York 10004
www.mla.org

To order MLA publications, visit www.mla.org/books. For wholesale and international orders, see www.mla.org/bookstore-orders. The EU-based Responsible Person for MLA products is the Mare Nostrum Group, which can be reached at gpsr@mare-nostrum.co.uk or the Mare Nostrum Group BV, Mauritskade 21D, 1091 GC Amsterdam, Netherlands. For a copy of the MLA's risk assessment document, write to scholcomm@mla.org.

Cover illustration: Raphaël Arnaud. Photograph of performance of *Iphis et Iante*, directed by Jean-Pierre Vincent, Théâtre du Gymnase, Marseille, 2013.

Cover description: The cover of this book features a photo from a performance of the play. The photo shows the two main characters on a bed, their faces close together as if they are about to kiss.

Texts and Translations 47
ISSN 1079-2538

Library of Congress Cataloging-in-Publication Data

Names: Benserade, Isaac de, 1613-1691, author. | Legault, Marianne, editor. | Adl, Ramine, translator. | Ovid, 43 B.C.-17 A.D. or 18 A.D. Metamorphoses.
Title: Iphis and Iante : a play based on Ovid's Metamorphoses / Isaac de Benserade edited by Marianne Legault ; translated by Ramine Adl.
Other titles: Iphis et Iante. English
Description: New York : The Modern Language Association of America, 2025.
Series: Texts and translations, 1079-2538 ; 47 | Includes bibliographical references.
Identifiers: LCCN 2025005897 (print) | LCCN 2025005898 (ebook) | ISBN 9781603296991 (paperback) | ISBN 9781603297004 (EPUB)
Subjects: LCGFT: Comedy plays. | Lesbian drama.
Classification: LCC PQ1715 .A6713 2025 (print) | LCC PQ1715 (ebook) | DDC 842/.4—dc23/eng/20250228
LC record available at https://lccn.loc.gov/2025005897
LC ebook record available at https://lccn.loc.gov/2025005898

Contents

Introduction

The story of a young man deeply in love with the woman he longs to marry has been a recurring motif in Western literature for centuries. Early modern French comedy is no exception: after all, what is a French comedy in the seventeenth century but a plot centered on an attempt to remove obstacles that prevent two young lovers from finding their happily-ever-after ending? Take, for example, Molière, acknowledged as one of the most masterful playwrights of French classical comedies. In many of Molière's plays a young couple's future happiness is threatened by an unreasonable father or guardian who puts his own desire (usually for money or elevated social status) above his children's happiness.[1] The plot will then focus on how to circumvent this irrational authority figure and bring about the long-awaited union of the two lovers. For, in the end, after all the commotion, a comedy must conclude with a marriage celebration and a return to familial and therefore social harmony. Such is the fabric of classical comedies in France during the second half of the seventeenth century, when the genre had reached its peak in popularity.

In the first half of the century, however, playwrights had more creative and literary freedom under the period's baroque aesthetic before the genre of the comedy became dictated by the classical rules of the three unities of time, place, and action (the story must take place within the span of a day, have one location, and have only one plot), and also by the notions of *vraisemblance* ("what should be believable") and *bienséance* ("decorum"). A baroque comedy could thus be allowed to explore all avenues, invite all possibilities, and offer spectacular and unanticipated solutions to its plot: the famous deus ex machina ("the god from the machine"; an ancient Greek and Roman dramatic term indicating when a god is suddenly introduced to resolve a plot that seemed otherwise unsolvable), to the delight of the spectators. While the story of the two young lovers' struggles and eventual union was still the very essence of French comedies during the baroque period, Isaac de Benserade's 1634 play, *Iphis et Iante* (*Iphis and Iante*), featured the absolute unexpected: a central love relationship between two young women, a plot that Benserade offered to an eager audience at the Hôtel de Bourgogne's theater in the heart of Paris.[2]

Born in Normandy in 1612 or 1613,[3] Benserade began his studies in philosophy. He left his scholarly pursuits in 1636 at the age of twenty-three after falling in love with a beautiful actress, Nicole Gassot, the wife of the well-known director Pierre Le Messier, known as Bellerose (Pawlowski 2), ultimately writing for her his first tragedy, *Cléopâtre*, which turned out to be his first real success. He dedicated this first published play to Cardinal Richelieu, a famous patron of the arts and an influential figure at the court of both Louis XIII and his son, the future king, Louis XIV. In recognition of his dedication and talent, Benserade obtained a regular pension from the cardinal until Richelieu's death in 1643. Although Benserade wrote a series of plays[4] under the cardinal's patronage, it is primarily his poetry and numerous ballets written between 1647 and 1680 that brought him recognition and acclaim. Encouraged by the cardinal's support, Benserade became a regular courtier at the court of Louis XIV. He collaborated on many ballets with the Italian-born French baroque composer Jean-Baptiste Lully, a favorite composer of

Louis XIV who wrote the music for most of the royal festivities and operas. The king was particularly fond of Benserade's ballets; in fact, Benserade is believed to have written the first ballet in which the young king appeared as a dancer, *Ballet de Cassandre* (*Cassandra*). Only thirteen years old at the time and dressed in a magnificent golden costume, the young Louis would come to be known thereafter as "le Roi soleil" ("the Sun King"; Duncan Jones 73–74). In the years that followed, Benserade went on to write many ballets in which the king took center stage, to the delight of courtiers.[5]

A familiar presence at the court of Louis XIV, Benserade was also a frequent visitor in elite *salons précieux* in Paris, such as the Chambre Bleue d'Arthénice ("Blue Room of Arthénice") where some of the most renowned poets and novelists gathered to exchange, discuss, and criticize one another's work, often still in progress.[6] It was in the famous Chambre Bleue, for instance, that he and the poet Vincent Voiture often enjoyed a friendly rivalry around newly created *précieux* stanzas in front of their peers. The *précieux* movement, born at the beginning of the seventeenth century and active until the mid-1660s, was designed to reform and refine the language and the social mores of French courtly and aristocratic societies.[7] To that end, *préciosité* encouraged the production and criticism of French literature and the pursuit of intellectuality, particularly when it came to women. Indeed, in the peak years of *préciosité* (1640–50), the social and intellectual status of women in the salons became greatly elevated because women were suddenly propelled into the role of being the ultimate judges of good taste, manners, and literary production. For a short time, women enjoyed an unusual intellectual and social power in these micro, elite communities hosted by writers such as Marie-Madeleine Pioche de la Vergne, known as Madame de La Fayette, and Madeleine de Scudéry (Beasley 41).[8]

It is within the context of the *précieux* movement—its preoccupation with love, its focus on women, and its quest for a more refined language—that Benserade's *Iphis and Iante* was written. The play combines *précieux* style (refinement and elegance) and baroque aesthetic, which often displays themes of illusion, disguise, humor, and misunderstanding as well as a taste for the spectacular, all of which are prominent in Benserade's comedy featuring a young woman who lives as a man.[9] Also important for Benserade's play is the notion of literary license, which is at the very core of baroque literary aesthetic but would later give way to the more sober and rigid classical taste of the second half of the century. The relative freedom afforded by the baroque years allowed the overt display onstage of physical love between two women in *Iphis and Iante.*

But how could a playwright safely portray same-sex love in 1634 without risking public disapproval or even his career? Spectators were likely to have been very familiar with the story of Iphis.[10] Indeed, Benserade recreates the plot laid out in the ninth book of the *Metamorphoses* by the Roman poet Ovid: from the day Iphis is born, her mother dresses her and raises her as a boy in order to save Iphis's life. Not wanting any financial burden associated with having a daughter, Iphis's father had made his wife promise him that she would kill the child at birth if it were a girl. Following those fatal instructions, however, Iphis's mother received assurance from the Egyptian goddess Isis that all would end well and that she should let the newborn infant live. Consequentially, the mother decides to trust in Isis.[11] Years later, Iphis falls in love with a young woman, Iante, and their families decide that it is time to marry the two young lovers. No one but the mother knows that Iphis is a young woman, and as the day of the wedding draws near, Iphis begins to feel tormented and ashamed of her "monstrous passion"; she eventually begs the gods to rescue her from her "senseless, stupid passion" (Ovid 163).

At the last moment, Isis appears and transforms Iphis into a young man. The transformation leaves no doubt of her sex, as emphasized in Ovid's description of her suddenly walking with "longer strides than she usually did, her face was not as fair, she seemed stronger, her features were sharper, her hair was shorter and uncombed, and she had more vigor than a female usually does" (264). Following Iphis's metamorphosis and a return to so-called "natural" law, the wedding can take place. Such is the well-known plot of *Iphis and Iante* that awaited the Parisian audience of 1634.

Little is known about the public's reception of this bold play when it was first performed in April 1634. According to a none-too-modest Benserade himself, it "[n]'a point paru tout à fait désagréable" ("it didn't appear to be at all unpleasant"; Pawlowski 2; our trans.) for the public. We also know, from the well-known seventeenth-century religious figure and scholar Paul Tallemant, that Benserade's comedy had relatively good success (Verdier 18). Despite what seems to have been a rather notable first attempt at a comedy, there is limited documentation about the play's reception. All that remains are the notes of the Hôtel de Bourgogne's stage designer, Laurent Mahelot,[12] who details the decor of the comedy in his memoirs:

> Au milieu du théâtre, il faut un temple fort superbe enrichy de tout ce que l'on peu. Au dessus du théâtre, une nue où est la déesse, et, dans le temple, parest le tableau de la déesse. Il faut, à costé du théâtre, une belle salle élevée, frise, ballustres et portique tappicer ; une table, un tapy, des chandeliers, deux sièges. Il faut un poignard, un tonnerre au mitan du cinquiesme acte. L'autre costé du théâtre à la fantaisie du feinteur. Le temple est fermé jusqu'au cinquiesme acte et s'ouvre au milieu de l'acte. Il faut une barbe pour la métamorphose, qui se colle au menton ; plus, une couronne

> d'épics, un croissant et un sceptre pour la déesse Isis, et c'est tout. (Mahelot and Laurent 36)

> In the center of the stage, there must be a most magnificent temple, richly adorned with all that can be found. Suspended above, a cloud where the goddess is and, in the temple, a portrait of the goddess is displayed. To the side of the stage there must be a beautiful raised room, a border, balusters, and a decorated portico; a table, a rug, candleholders, two seats. A dagger is needed, thunder in the middle of the fifth act. The other side of the stage is left to the decorator's fancy. The temple remains closed until the fifth act and opens in the middle of the act. A beard, which sticks to the chin, is needed for the metamorphosis; also, a crown of thorns, a crescent and a scepter for the goddess Isis, and that is all. (our trans.)

In addition to Mahelot's account, we know that the stage would have been lit by a row of candles and chandeliers laid out on the floor, according to the scenic practice at the time. Nothing is known about the specific actors who featured in Benserade's comedy. However, women were allowed to act in early modern French dramas, including in comedies, unlike in Shakespeare's plays. Furthermore, it is important to note that throughout the play, Iphis never sees herself as a man. We can therefore reasonably deduce that the role of the young woman Iphis most likely was played by a woman, thus staying true to the play's central plot: the experience of a young woman in love with someone of the same sex.

Benserade makes significant changes to the original Ovidian story that affect the ways in which the passion between the two women is represented onstage. First, he ages the character of Iphis so that she is no longer an adolescent girl but a young woman of twenty (Biet 68). This maturity allows

Benserade to fully explore the erotic passion and sexual attraction of Iphis for Iante, as we witness when Iphis tells her mother about her desires—"Ainsi que sa beauté, mes feux sont infinis" ("Her beauty is infinite, as is my burning fire"; 1.2)[13]—and also when she confides in her friend Ergaste the seductive power that Iante holds over her senses: "Sa beauté me ravit" ("Her beauty delights me"; 2.5). Secondly, in Benserade, the metamorphosis of Iphis into a man occurs the day *after* her wedding to Iante and not before, as is the case in Ovid's plot. These two changes provide an important variation in the representation of erotic love between the two women, one that not only reveals the possibility of such love but also explores its emotional and sexual dimensions. Indeed, and unexpectedly, Benserade's narrative openly displays the depths of Iphis's erotic desire for Iante, as seen in act 5 when Iphis relates to her mother the passion and the pleasure she felt during their wedding night: "J'embrassais ce beau corps dont la blancheur extrême / M'excitait à lui faire une place en moi-même. / Je touchais, je baisais, j'avais le cœur content" ("I embraced her beautiful body whose extreme whiteness / Aroused me to make room for her within myself. / I touched; I kissed; my heart was happy"; 5.4). Clearly, the playwright does not shy away from representing the young woman's erotic bliss. Through Iphis's description of consummating the wedding night, Benserade offers the first representation of lesbian love in the history of French comedy. Although Ovid recognizes Sapphic love in his *Metamorphoses*, it appears only through the lens of the shame and denaturalization felt by Iphis. Thus, despite conceiving of the possibility of same-sex love between women, Ovid gives his female lovers no avenue of expression and no freedom to physically experience their love. In Ovid, Iphis's passion for Iante is limited to being a tragic affair, a stark contrast to Benserade's comedy.

The theme of same-sex love in Benserade's play is not restricted to women. In a third modification of Ovid's plot, the playwright also introduces the concept of male homoerotic desire through the addition of three new characters: the bachelor Ergaste, who is in love with Iphis; Nise, Ergaste's confidant and friend; and Mérinte, Nise's sister, who in turn loves Ergaste. Benserade uses these characters to develop a secondary homosexual love plot. Within this subplot, while Ergaste knows of Iphis's real sexual identity, no one else in the play does, including Nise and Mérinte. Consequently, when Nise suggests a marriage between Ergaste and his sister Mérinte, Ergaste flatly refuses and instead divulges his love for Iphis to his friend: "Tu vois que j'aime Iphis autant qu'on peut aimer / . . . / Je le tiens préférable aux plus belles du monde" ("You see that I love Iphis as much as one can love / . . . / I think him preferable to the world's most beautiful women"; 2.2). This is the first of many confessions of love that he professes. Henceforth, when Ergaste pines openly for Iphis, the play's other characters are left wondering about his state of mind, given that it appears to them that he is attracted to a man. All the characters, with the exception of Iphis, her mother, and Ergaste himself, thus see the love-struck Ergaste and his obsession with Iphis as a sign of folly, which of course enhances the comic elements of the play.

Finally, Benserade's portrayal of the love between Iphis and Iante is not only groundbreaking for the time, it is also relatively compassionate when compared to Ovid's, insofar as their love is fully reciprocated. Indeed, Iante's love for Iphis does not diminish even after the revelation on the wedding night in the last act: "Ce mariage est doux ; j'y trouve assez d'appâts / Et si l'on n'en riait, je ne m'en plaindrais pas" ("This marriage is sweet, I find it attractive enough / And if people did not laugh, I would not complain"; (5.1). Iante is thus not put off by the discovery of Iphis's sex, and, rather than being outraged at Iphis's trickery, she simply worries about the social embarrassment such a union would bring. In contrast to the positive portrayal of Iphis and Iante's love, heterosexual relationships are portrayed as either unrequited—the young Mérinte loves Ergaste, who, in turn, pines only for Iphis, who loves Iante—or extremely problematic—Ligde, the cruel husband, who orders his wife to murder their newborn child. The celebration of love, a recurring theme in comedies, is given an ideal representation in this play by the lesbian couple. Although avant-garde, this staging of lesbian love could only take place within the fabric of the baroque comedy, especially given that lesbians had been represented as threatening in France since the Renaissance.

These major modifications of the original Ovidian plot enabled Benserade to stage same-sex love, and especially lesbian love, which remains front and center in his play. This is an innovative endeavor in the history of early modern French literature. Readers might question to what extent we can speak of the modern concepts of sexual identity and lesbian love as they pertain to seventeenth-century France. Many historians and literary critics have argued that the term and the representations of its practice do not circulate in French literature until the eighteenth century.[14] However, a closer look into dictionaries and treatises of early modern France tells a different story.[15] Same-sex love between women remained without a specific name in France for a long time. To speak of sexual relationships between women, the Middle Ages used the term "péché de luxure" ("sin of debauchery"; our trans.), which largely encompassed any sexual pleasure enjoyed outside the bonds of marriage (Bonnet 34). It was not until the second half of the Renaissance that a woman engaging in same-sex relationships obtained a distinct name: *la tribade*. By that time, female same-sex relations had acquired a threatening dimension.[16] The term *tribade* appears for the first time in France in Henri Estienne's 1566 treatise, *Introduction au traité de la conformité des merveilles anciennes avec les modernes (Introduction to the Treatise on the Conformity between Ancient Wonders and Modern Ones)*, and more specifically in the chapter "Du péché de sodomie et du péché contre nature en nostre temps" ("On the sin of sodomy and on sinning against nature in our times"; Bonnet 29). In this definition, the tribade is guilty of "meschanceté" ("maliciousness"; our trans.; Bonnet 31)—that is to say, of dressing up as a man and of penetration, a crime punishable by death by fire. The real offense according to Estienne is not that the tribade has loved another woman but that she has loved her while in a masculine disguise and that she has appropriated the phallus by imitating the function of a man.[17] Estienne's understanding of a tribade is thus a "vilaine" ("wicked woman"; our trans.) worthy of her deadly punishment. In the seventeenth century, Pierre de Bourdeille, seigneur de Brantôme, continues this representation of the male-imitating tribade in his *Vies des dames galantes (Lives of Gallant Ladies)*:[18]

> On dit que Sapho de Lesbos a esté fort bonne maitresse en ce mestier, voire, dit-on, qu'elle l'a inventé, et que depuis les dames lesbiennes l'ont imitée en cela et continué jusques aujourd'huy . . . telles femmes sont les femmes de Lesbos, qui ne veulent pas souffrir les hommes, mais s'approchent des autres femmes ainsi que les hommes eux-mesmes. (121)

> It is said that Sapho of Lesbos was a mighty mistress of this occupation, even, it is said, that she invented it, and that since then, lesbian ladies have imitated her and continue to do so until today . . . such women are the women of Lesbos, who do not want to be near men, but who go near other women just as men themselves do. (our trans.)

In addition to the familiar motif of the female lover imitating a man, Brantôme's use of the term "lesbian" enables our inclusion of it in the introduction despite the play's early modern context.

What is striking about Benserade's depiction of Iphis is that she is kind, gentle, and sweet—in other words, completely unthreatening. At no point does Iphis attempt to confer upon herself phallic, and therefore threatening, behaviors, in contrast to the definition of lesbian according to Brantôme. Not only is Iphis not represented as virile, on the contrary, she is portrayed as an incomplete being because she lacks a phallus; Iphis laments her shortcomings in making Iante her wife throughout the play, that is, her inability to consummate heterosexual sex.

This emphasis on Iphis's lack of a phallus is key to the comedic aspect of the play: the emotional dissociation between Iphis, who is preoccupied with her pain or obsession, and the audience, who sees that preoccupation as foolish. From the beginning to the end of the play, Iphis's incompleteness as a lover drives the plot. Whether lamented by Iphis's mother, Télétuze, or by Iphis herself, her inability to complete "les fonctions d'un homme" ("the duties of a man"; 1.1) is constantly highlighted.[19] As the wedding night approaches, Iphis attempts to disclose the truth to Iante in terms that clearly reveal her feelings of inadequacy. She sees herself as "incapable" ("unfit") and "imparfait" ("imperfect"; 2.3). Iphis's obsession with her own lack of phallus culminates on the night of the wedding in a long soliloquy that highlights the deficiency in her passion for Iante: "Quoi! Je m'endormirais auprès de cette belle / Et je ne ferais pas l'impossible pour elle ? / Je serais inutile en un si digne emploi ?" ("What! I would fall asleep next to this beauty / And would not do the impossible for her? / I would be useless in such a worthy cause?"; 2.6). Benserade thus delights his spectators with the comic trope of Iphis's lack. Pun after pun, the audience comes to see the young woman as a desperate lover in need of a miraculous remedy. For all those aware of how the story ends, the audience's potential discomfort with the play's lesbian character is quickly averted. Isis keeps her promise, and Iphis becomes a man at the last moment, before attempting to kill herself with a knife.[20] The lesbian is repatriated within heterosexual norms, and the social order is finally reinstated. What began as an impossible situation can now end in a celebration of love and life (to come), one where the play, in the final scene of act 5, quickly erases all traces of the first wedding night: "Et ce n'est qu'aujourd'hui qu'hymen unit nos cœurs. / . . . / Et la seconde nuit doit être la première" ("And it is only today that marriage unites our hearts. / . . . / And our second night must be our first"). All's well that ends well. Iphis's last words underscore a newly acquired virility:

> Si vous ne jugez pas mes discours véritables,
> Je vous en ferai voir des effets bien palpables
> Et ma chère moitié d'une bonne façon
> Prouvera dans neuf mois qu'Iphis est un garçon.
>
> If you do not judge my words to be truthful
> I will show you some very palpable results
> And my dear half will convincingly
> Prove, in nine months, that Iphis is a man.[21]

Although nearly four hundred years old, *Iphis and Iante* holds new interest for readers today, when issues of gender representations and gender fluidity have become increasingly influential in contemporary study and discourse. In addition to the theme of same-sex love, readers may interpret the final metamorphosis as an instance of gender transformation. Indeed, modern readers may find the comedy's treatment of lesbian love and the final metamorphosis of the young woman into a man make *Iphis and Iante* surprisingly queer for an early modern play. Given current and emerging questions and discussions surrounding gender identity, queer love, social norms, and nonbinary identities, it is our hope that Benserade's avant-garde comedy can finally grow its readership and obtain its overdue literary recognition among scholars and students alike.

Notes

1. *Les Précieuses ridicules*, Molière's first successful comedy, and *Dom Juan* are examples of exceptions to this plot.

2. The theater of the Hôtel de Bourgogne was built in 1548. In the seventeenth century, it hosted many plays by Racine, Molière, and Corneille.

3. Scholars and biographers are divided on the exact year and place where Benserade was born. Most identify Lyons-la-Fôret in Normandy as the birthplace. Some, however, claim he was born in the Marais district in Paris.

4. Following the success of *Cléopâtre*, Benserade published *Iphis et Iante* (Paris, 1637), *La mort d'Achille et la dispute de ses armes* (*The Death of Achilles and the Quarrel of His Weapons*; Paris, 1637), *Gustave ou l'heureuse ambition* (*Gustave or the Lucky Ambition*; Paris, 1637), and *Méléagre* (Paris, 1640).

5. Between 1654 and 1669, Benserade wrote a series of ballets in which the king performed. For a detailed list, see Maupoint 51–65.

6. Arthénice is an anagram for Catherine de Rambouillet, an aristocrat and lover of literature who created a *salon*, a space at l'Hôtel de Rambouillet from around 1620 to 1648 where contemporary writers and nobles could mingle and discuss literary creations. The Chambre Bleue is also referred to as the Salon de la Marquise de Rambouillet.

7. For more on the history of the *préciosité*, see Beasley; Duchêne; Maître; and Backer.

8. As Beasley notes, by the 1650s, however, the terms *précieux* and *préciosité* began to acquire negative connotations. A famous example of this is Molière's satire *Les Précieuses ridicules*.

9. For more on how Benserade constructs a distinctly baroque lesbian character, see Legault.

10. Ovid's *Metamorphoses* was well known during the seventeenth century. Jean Jehasse explains that "les jeunes gens s'y frottent de latin, les Mondains continuent de déchiffrer le monde grâce à cette 'théologie des Païens' qui inspire et illustre les arts et les manifestations de la vie de cour" ("young people use it to try their hands at Latin, socialites continue to unravel the world thanks to this 'Pagan theology' which inspires and illustrates the arts and events of courtly life"; 325; our trans.). Benserade would return to Ovid's *Metamorphoses* later on in his career when he translated it in his *Metamorphoses d'Ovide en rondeaux* (*Ovid's Metamorphoses in Rondeaux*).

11. The Egyptian mother goddess Isis was revered by the ancient Greeks and Romans for her fertility powers.

12. Mahelot was a stage designer at the Hôtel de Bourgogne from 1622 to 1635 (Pawlowski 2).

13. Translations from the play are by Marianne Legault and Ramine Adl.

14. See Waelti-Walters's *Damned Women*, for example, in which the author retraces the birth of lesbianism in French literature to Denis Diderot's *La Religieuse* (*The Nun*, 1796).

15. The history of lesbian representations in France is a curious one; attempts at defining the figure of the lesbian range from the Ovidian tradition of the abandoned, older, and grief-stricken Sappho to the dangerous, male-imitating tribade.

16. For more on the threatening dimensions of the tribade in early modern Europe, see Traub.

17. Wahl demonstrates the "cultural anxiety" that emerges in early modern France around the male-imitating tribade (21–23).

18. Written around the 1590s, *Gallant Ladies* was not published until 1666, more than fifty years after Brantôme's death in 1614.

19. Benserade would later return to the theme of the lesbian without a phallus in his poem "Sur l'Amour d'Uranie avec Philis" ("On Uranie's Love with Philis"; *Poésie*).

20. The suicide attempt with the knife may be seen as a metaphor for procuring the phallus that Iphis lacks yet so desires. In its absence, she suggests that she will die by it symbolically.

21. Stanton reminds us of the pressure on early modern males to prove their masculinity by showing evidence of "their potency and capacity to engender" (8).

Works Cited

Backer, Dorothy A. *Precious Women*. Basic Books, 1974.

Beasley, Faith E. *Salons, History, and the Creation of Seventeenth-Century France*. Ashgate, 2006.

Benserade, Isaac de. *Ballet de Cassandre*. Paris, 1651. *Gallica*, gallica.bnf.fr/ark:/12148/bpt6k72564h.

———. *Cléopâtre*. Paris, 1636. *Gallica*, gallica.bnf.fr/ark:/12148/bpt6k71387c.

———. *Metamorphoses d'Ovide en rondeaux*. Imprimerie royale, 1676.

———. "Sur l'Amour d'Uranie avec Philis." 1697. *Poésie*. Slatkine Reprints, 1967, pp. 165–73.

Biet, Christian. "À quoi rêvent les jeunes filles? Homosexualité féminine, travestissement et comédie: Le cas d'*Iphis et Iante* de Benserade (1634)." *La femme au XVIIe siècle: Actes du colloque de Vancouver, University of British Columbia, 5–7 octobre 2000*, edited by Richard Hodgson, *Biblio 17*, no. 138, 2022, pp. 53–81.

Bonnet, Marie-Jo. *Les relations amoureuses entre femmes du XVIe au XXe siècles*. Éditions Odile Jacob, 1995.

Brantôme, Pierre de Bourdeille. *Les vies des dames galantes*. 1666. Edited by Maurice Rat, Le Livre de Poche, 1962.

Diderot, Denis. *La Religieuse*. Paris, 1796.

Duchêne, Roger. *Les Précieuses ou comment l'esprit vint aux femmes*. Fayard, 2001.

Duncan Jones, E. E. "Notes and Documents: Dryden, Benserade, and Marvell." *Huntington Library Quarterly*, vol. 54, no. 1, winter 1991, pp. 73–78.

Estienne, Henri. *Introduction au traité de la conformité des merveilles anciennes avec les modernes*. Geneva, 1566.

Jehasse, Jean. "De la fable aux fables: Benserade et La Fontaine." *Mélanges offerts à Georges Couton*, PU de Lyon, 1981, pp. 323–44.

Legault, Marianne. "*Iphis and Iante*: Traumatisme de l'incomplétude lesbienne au Grand Siècle." *Representations of Trauma in French and Francophone Literature*, edited by Nicole Simek and Zahi Zalloua, special issue of *Dalhousie French Studies*, no. 81, winter 2007, pp. 83–93.

Mahelot, Laurent, and Michel Laurent. *La mise en scène à Paris au XVIIe siècle: Mémoire de Laurent Mahelot et Michel Laurent*. Edited by Émile Dacier, Société de l'Histoire de Paris et de l'Île de France, 1901.

Maître, Myriam. *Les Précieuses. Naissance des femmes de lettres en France au XVIIe siècle*. Champion, 1999.

Maupoint. *Bibliothèque des théâtres, contenant le catalogue alphabétique des pièces dramatiques et opéra, le nom des auteurs et le temps de la représentation de ces pièces, avec des anecdotes sur les auteurs et sur la plupart des pièces contenues en ce recueil*. Pierre Prault, 1733.

Molière. *Dom Juan ou Le Festin de pierre*. Paris, 1665.

———. *Les Précieuses ridicules*. Paris, 1659.

Ovid. *The Metamorphoses of Ovid*. Translated by Michael Simpson, U of Massachusetts P, 2001.

Pawlowski, Gaston de. "Benserade, auteur tragique." *Comoedia*, 9 Aug. 1925, p. 2. *Gallica*, gallica.bnf.fr/ark:/12148/bpt6k76498312/f2.item.r=iphis%20et%20iante%20benserade.

Stanton, Domna. *The Dynamics of Gender in Early Modern France*. Ashgate, 2014.

Traub, Valerie. *The Renaissance of Lesbianism in Early Modern England*. Cambridge UP, 2002.

Verdier, Anne. Préface. *Iphis et Iante*, by Isaac de Benserade, edited by Verdier, Lampsaque, 2000, pp. 7–33.

Waelti-Walters, Jennifer. *Damned Women: Lesbians in French Novels*. McGill UP, 2000.

Wahl, Susan Elizabeth. *Invisible Relations: Representations of Female Intimacy in the Age of Enlightenment*. Stanford UP, 1999.

Note on the Translation

In producing an English translation of *Iphis and Iante*, our goal has been to make Benserade's play accessible to undergraduate students and general readers. Our approach to the translation has been to stay as close as possible to Benserade's phrasing in French while striving for a natural expression of the text in English free verse. As in the French edition, we have followed contemporary norms for punctuation and the use of capital letters, except in some cases such as with "Love," "Hymen," and "Fortune" where the author refers to the gods. We hope to have produced a readable text in contemporary English that retains the tone and spirit of the original comedy. There are several instances where the meaning of a phrase or passage is ambiguous in the original French. Generally, we have tried not to resolve ambiguities present in the original French dialogue unless we felt it was necessary to make the situation clear for the reader. We have also added explanatory footnotes whenever a clarification seemed necessary.

French editions of the play follow a twelve-syllable alexandrine verse structure. In an alexandrine, a single line number may apply to two or more lines of text, presented with indentations, signifying the continuation of a single line of verse. We have kept this convention in the translation even though we have chosen to translate it in free verse. The indentations have no poetic value but assist with the reading of the play because they indicate the presence of an alexandrine in the French and align approximately with the line numbering in the original edition. Readers should note that the line numbering in the English translation does not always correspond to the French text; in the translation, in order to present a natural syntax in English, we have occasionally transposed two lines, as in the following:

SŒUR D'ERGASTE	ERGASTE'S SISTER
Ergaste, mon ami, si jamais ton courage	Ergaste, my friend, if ever your courage
S'est fait paraître ferme au milieu d'un orage,	Has stood firmly in the midst of a storm,
Si jamais ton esprit s'est montré généreux	If your heart has ever shown generosity
Et si tu fus jamais et sage et malheureux	And if ever you have been wise and unhappy,
Dans les afflictions que le ciel te prépare,	Let us now see your rare steadfastness
Tu nous peux témoigner une constance rare.	**Amid the afflictions that the gods are preparing for you.**

Iphis and Iante

Introductory Epistle

Dear Sir,

My Lord Bautru,

Presenter of ambassadors, etc.

Sir,

I do not aim hereby to declare my indebtedness to you; it is rather a pure homage that I render to the most perfect mind at court, who is so generally respected that to receive the glory of its approbation must be the ultimate goal of the best works—not that I offer you this first attempt as such, for to offer you less than a masterpiece would cause you embarrassment. Having surveyed the whole of France, I have found no virtue greater than yours, nor one that shines brighter of its own merit. And I believe that antiquity would have been at fault not to adore you and make of you one of its gods; you, whose incomparable goodness extends indifferently to all kinds of people, so that one can say rightly that Fortune has indeed looked after every one when she was working for you alone. Thus, Sir, without flattering you, I hold that there are few like you, who truly are what they appear to be, especially in these times when self-interest weaves itself into the most heroic actions of our lives and where concealment, winsome and subtle, imperceptibly usurps the name of that ancient honesty that died out during the early centuries and that we have forgotten a long time ago. It is quite true that in providing for others, you also provide for yourself, as it is so natural for you to offer help that you can let no such opportunity pass without offending yourself and going against your own noble and generous inclination. As for me, I have felt directly and continue to feel, every day, the effects of it, which places me in the rank of those who bear witness to a publicly known fact. If it holds that for a destitute person to acknowledge a debt counts as a half payment, then I am not entirely without hope to acquit myself of my obligation in full. If not, I must die tainted with the darkest of vices and perish miserably among the mass of the ungrateful. Allow me, please, Sir, to openly publish my sincere appreciation for the honor that you do me and believe that I remain,

Sir,
Your humble and devoted servant,
De Benserade

To the Reader

This small note is to inform you of something that you may know just as well as I do, which is that this comedy is taken from the ninth book of Ovid's *Metamorphoses*, and that it is actually a metamorphosis that I have adapted for the theater. The sterility of the subject matter forced me to stitch together a few story lines whose arrangement and flow did not seem to me entirely distasteful. I do not aspire to equal Ovid in his glory; it will mean much to me if I did not make him blush. You will be the judge of that. Goodbye. Overlook the printing errors, if there are any, and forgive mine.

Dramatis Personae

IPHIS, a young woman dressed as a young man

IANTE, Iphis's fiancée

TÉLESTE, Iante's father

LIGDE, Iphis's father

TÉLÉTUZE, Iphis's mother

ERGASTE'S SISTER, Télétuze's confidante

ERGASTE, in love with Iphis

NISE, Ergaste's friend

MÉRINTE, in love with Ergaste, Nise's sister

TÉLESTE'S SERVANT

THE GODDESS ISIS[1]

The setting is in Crete.

Vota puer solvit quae foemina voverat Iphis.[2]
(9 lib. Met. Ovid.)

1. Egyptian goddess of fertility.

2. "Iphis the boy made good on the vows which he as a girl had made." We thank Michael Treschow for this translation. Ovid's *Metamorphoses* uses "dona puer" ("a gift") and not "vota puer" ("vows"), as it appears in Benserade's text.

Act 1

Scene 1

Ligde, Télétuze, Iphis

LIGDE

Why this mood? What repulses you
And makes you delay this fortunate union?
Why exert yourself to prevent its due course?
Is it not conducive to our lasting peace of mind?
Are you displeased with the wealth brought by this match?
Does it not provide comfortably for a son?

TÉLÉTUZE

You think only of wealth.

LIGDE

And what else would you like
My heart to settle on to bring out her virtue?
Would you like it to linger on the choice of a face?
You cannot forge a good marriage without wealth.
His young heart's privilege is to love what he likes
And ours is to love his interests.

Your noble sentiments are out of fashion:
One flees poverty because it is troublesome.
All other afflictions are fed by that evil;
It cannot fool you with glints of false riches
And most especially in our times
When gold has set up altars in the minds of men
And the desire for gain, ease, and happiness
Raises this treacherous metal above honor.
As long as riches come along with a girl,
She is seen as beautiful, respectable, and from a good family.
While the purse is flush and gold holds its course,
Virtues keep increasing day by day.
Besides, the beautiful Iante is as well-behaved as she is rich
And her father is not considered to be a penny pincher.
He is well regarded and has a good income
And his worth is so great as to be known by all.
Will we not be grateful for our prosperous fate
When our own son, in turn, becomes our father?
And will we not be thankful for our happy destiny,
Receiving from our son what he acquired through us?
What support should we expect in our old age
If my son refused the honor of becoming his son-in-law?

TÉLÉTUZE

It is all very well to ensure our future peace of mind[3]

3. In the original, Benserade uses *repos*, an important seventeenth-century literary concept referring to a peaceful state of being.

But we must also provide for that of our children.
Iphis is still young and while he adores Iante,
I do not think his love is a passionate one.

LIGDE

You speak without cause. Do you not see, then,
How Iphis fawns upon her and how he pines for her charms?
How Iante returns the affection he sends her way
And how she appears to be contented by it all?
Do you not perceive in the words they exchange
Their mutual love, visible on their faces?

TÉLÉTUZE

I see it all too well, but . . .

LIGDE

But what?

TÉLÉTUZE

It seems to me
That they will never be suited to each other.
Bound by Venus's laws, these lovers
Will be unable to love each other when better acquainted.
I grant that they like each other, that they are the same age,
But they lack what they need to make a good household.

LIGDE

What do they lack?

TÉLÉTUZE

The maturity, in this serious matter,
To bear without complaint such a heavy burden.
Iphis is just a child, consumed by the weakest flame,
and could not fulfill the duties of a man.

LIGDE

Do you jest? To still count Iphis among the children?
A young man such as him, twenty years of age?

TÉLÉTUZE

It is true that he is in the prime of his youth
Yet, for one to marry, one needs more than that.
One must be fully formed before getting tangled
In a knot from which one can never be torn.
How a young man suffers and how he despairs
When his own children reach the age of their father;
And when, too soon, his heirs become unpleasant
To see him still alive at the age of thirty!
To prevent such blame, my dear, let us avoid
Losing him so soon by giving him a wife.

LIGDE

Well then, will you never do as I wish?
Let us speak of it no more; it is decided.
And since there is only your mind to oppose
All the good arguments that mine has proposed,
Today these lovers will exchange their vows

For I can be headstrong, just as much as you.
The father consents; the daughter is happy
And Iphis languishes in waiting, no doubt.
Their only desire is to be joined in marriage.

TÉLÉTUZE

And yet, I do not see them well suited for it.

LIGDE *to Iphis*

Is that so? Say something. This matter concerns you
Yet you care not, it seems, to open your mouth.
Do you not love Iante and are you not ready
To follow my will as you would a decree?

IPHIS *answers coldly*

Iante holds my soul in her complete power
And I only live to obey your wishes.

LIGDE

I expected no less from such a pleasant disposition
Which desires its own good and fears my anger.
My son, you deserve this young marvel
Whose rare beauty has never been equaled.
Look here, join in with the chatter a little
And see at once to preparing the banquet.
I will meet you tonight at her father's house
Where we will conclude the rest of this matter
So that tonight a chaste union will grant you
The means to taste the sweetness of its fruit.

Scene 2

Télétuze, Iphis

TÉLÉTUZE

Poor Iphis, is there anything quite like you?
How I pity the misfortune of your wretched destiny;
Fate is playing its hand, leading you to the point
Of fearing this marriage but not fleeing from it.
Your love makes you wish that the hour was nearer
But a hidden secret makes you fear its outcome.
I have done what I could to break up this contract.
I wanted to help you and if I did some harm,
Even if I stripped myself of motherly feelings,
I would join with you in your bitter suffering.
What hope do you have and what will you become?
Alas! Which way will your courage turn you?
This momentous day has come. Please, think of yourself:
Understand that despite my best efforts, you are to be married
And that your father, wielding absolute power,
Hurts you by granting what you want.
You cherish the beauty of the one given to you;
Your heart burns for her and that amazes me.
Think about your actions; control your passion;
Seek a more appropriate object for your affection.
Flee Iante's beauty; strive to distract yourself from it.
Being too much like you, she is harmful to you.

Stop worshipping her divine charms.
Neither nature nor the gods permit you to do so.
Without your account of the fire that you say burns in you,
I would think you were lying or, perhaps, pretending.
Do you, in fact, love her?

IPHIS

If it is not love,
Then I do not deserve the air that I breathe.
Yes, mother, I love her; and, whatever people say,
I feel, as any other, the agony of love.
Her beauty is infinite, as is my burning fire,
And a thousand times I wish to see our hearts united.

TÉLÉTUZE

But do you understand the object of your excessive love?
Or, to put it plainly, do you not know yourself?
You know who Iante is and that such a perfect gift,
Delightful as it is, is not fitting for you.
You know that, in the end, your fire will be as ice to her
When she discovers your flaws and sees her own charms.
Why do you allow your heart to keep burning
With a fire that real love has never set alight?

IPHIS

These are strange doings! And whoever knows this mystery
Is forced to marvel at it and stay silent.

TÉLÉTUZE

How I pity you, Iphis! And how we will soon see
The astonishing results of your blind fire!
You could delay this unhappy marriage
Which will forever be to your disadvantage.
In the end, this fiery passion is an illusion
And I fear it will turn to your confusion.

IPHIS

The gods will assist me and the good goddess
Will show us some effect from her old promise.
We must hope that the heavens are appeased
And will assist me in this present matter.
Meanwhile, I will go and see what is being done for the
nuptials
And what is being prepared for our celebration,
Since today is the day to conclude the contract
That I so desire and yet fear so much.
I leave you then, as your charming neighbor
Is coming this way to discuss things with you.

Scene 3

Ergaste's sister, Télétuze

ERGASTE'S SISTER

I was coming to see you to inquire
If we have cause to fear or to hope.

TÉLÉTUZE

Alas! All is lost, my dear confidante.
He absolutely wants Iphis to marry Iante.
For my part, I no longer dare speak of it.
My strongest arguments cannot sway his resolve.

ERGASTE'S SISTER

So the matter goes badly?

TÉLÉTUZE

I am deeply troubled by it
And wish that I had never gotten involved.
The marriage will be concluded and I received the insult
That in thinking to delay it, I hurried its course.
Knowing the man's temper, I should have
Pretended that my heart wanted this marriage.
To press him to give his consent
Would have been the best way to deter him from giving it.
Alas! What shall we do? How can we now hang
Any hope on mere appearances?
How unhappy I am! And such sorrow I'll have
If today my secret must be discovered!

ERGASTE'S SISTER

Today?

TÉLÉTUZE

I am now at the end of my schemes

And can no longer forge any new excuses.
For four or five months, I have been delaying
The astonishing result of this wretched love.
And now! Fate contrives to conclude the union;
My husband seeks it impatiently;
The girl is happy with it and, best of all,
Iphis . . .

ERGASTE'S SISTER

Delays it?

TÉLÉTUZE

On the contrary, agrees to it.

ERGASTE'S SISTER

O gods! Who has ever seen such a wonder!
And though they proceed with this extraordinary event,
What can come of it? Do we not know well
That all these fine projects will serve no purpose?
Those two are too alike to get along well.
The best part is lacking from their union.
One will be ashamed and the other vexed.
Chastity will make her throne of their bed.
If ties such as these united the whole world,
Would that not make nature fertile!
The immortals would no longer be offered incense
And this great universe would become a vast desert!
You can rightly set aside the fear that grips you:

A union like this will not be concluded.
Our young lovers can find no charm in it
And I expect that they will not want it.
I know them too well and though the young Iante
Burns in her feverish love for your Iphis,
A closer look at such a perfect lover,
And she will soon say: "that is not for me."
And when the elders will want to conclude the business,
Despite all their power, they cannot do enough
To make Iphis accept Iante in the role of husband.

TÉLÉTUZE

But they do not know the secret as we do.
Since Iphis agrees to it, who could forbid him
To marry a maiden and to pass as a son-in-law?
Our secrets[4] are hidden. They will not prevent
This amorous couple from reaching the final stage.
And then, how pitiful!

ERGASTE'S SISTER

There lies all the dread
That afflicts my soul, both for you and for them.
How these poor lovers are ill-suited!
How aptly they will be called the newlyweds![5]

4. "Secrets" refers to both the sexual identity of Iphis and how the truth has been concealed from others.

5. Ergaste's sister is playing with the concept of "newlyweds" here, as a new kind of marriage.

But let us find a way and the means to help us.
We must find an extreme remedy to this extreme plight.
Advise Iphis not to give her consent;
Ergaste and I, at least, will oppose it.
Here he comes, I think. This sad news
Will worry and trouble him, as it does us.

TÉLÉTUZE

Since he shares these secrets with us,
We can tell him the unfortunate turn of events
So he can put things in order, disrupt the celebrations,
Rather than suffer another to steal his conquest.
With due care, he can perhaps still keep for himself
The friend and mistress of whom he is to be deprived.

Scene 4

Ergaste's sister, Ergaste, Télétuze

ERGASTE'S SISTER

Ergaste, my friend, if ever your courage
Has stood firmly in the midst of a storm,
If your heart has ever shown generosity
And if ever you have been wise and unhappy,
Let us now see your rare steadfastness
Amid the afflictions that the gods are preparing for you.

ERGASTE

You know me well and you are not unaware of

How I behave during such trials.
You know with what countenance I submit to fortune,
What face I show when fate afflicts me
And whether I take any more heed
Of good, bad, comfort or affliction.
You know that my soul has long lost the habit
Of discerning the sweet from the bitter
And since the moment I have fallen in love,
I draw all of my contentment from being unhappy.
So, tell me everything: hide or conceal nothing
Since I learn every day to suffer silently.

ERGASTE'S SISTER

There is no lover under the laws of love
Who is less guilty and punished more than you.

ERGASTE

You make me languish in such impatience!
It hurts my soul a little and weighs on your conscience.
This turn of fate will be most harsh
If it pains me as much as your wordiness.

ERGASTE'S SISTER

Iphis . . .

ERGASTE

What of Iphis?

ERGASTE'S SISTER

Let others tell you the rest.
I do not wish to report such an ominous event
Nor to watch you receive, as an added burden,
News of your death sentence from your sister's lips.

ERGASTE

O gods! Tell me everything unless you wish
To see your brother die and expire on the spot!
I think I perceive the object of my grief
And I read on your face the signs of misfortune.
This turn of fate concerns Iphis. What odious traitor,
What hateful executioner has taken her beautiful soul?
Even if the heavens exerted this violent effort,
Tell me promptly; I will avenge her death.
Or, if my power is too weak in this moment,
Let me know of her death so that I can mourn it,
So I can gift her the last of my wishes
And so the same grave can enclose us both.
I have kept my life on her account;
Iphis having lost hers, let mine be taken.

TÉLÉTUZE

You are tormenting this poor lad too much.
Really, one should not make such a fuss:
Iphis is marrying Iante.

ERGASTE

Is that the great storm
That should overcome me? Ha! What a marriage!
How badly you know the art of upsetting me.
Rather than afflicting me, that makes me laugh!

TÉLÉTUZE

The time is past for laughter, Ergaste, I swear to you
That today the laws of nature are being breached.
If you love Iphis, as I believe you do,
Prevent this tragedy!

ERGASTE

You are joking!
Iphis marries Iante! How outrageous!
Who has ever witnessed such a union?
What an enchanting wedding! What a delightful husband!

TÉLÉTUZE

And yet, that is so.

ERGASTE

It does not make me jealous.
Although they are joined today in marriage
And they will be permitted to lie together,
I will love her no less for it afterwards
And I will have more hope than I ever had.
Such a misfortune affects me very little

And does not have the power to lessen my burning desire.
I have too much affection for two such beautiful lovers
And I take some pleasure in their satisfaction.
Let them freely taste the ambrosia of love.
I will never have cause to be jealous of it
And will always wish fate to be kind to them.
Let misfortune strike me if I want to hurt them!
They both burn with such a sincere flame
And are too innocent to commit a crime knowingly.

ERGASTE'S SISTER

While we are speaking, this couple is just about
To be joined, one to the other, today.
Both fathers have given their word
And nothing prevents them from concluding the marriage.

ERGASTE

Ha! How easily you contradict yourself!
Nothing prevents them from uniting these lovers?
Is their secret not known to you?

ERGASTE'S SISTER

It is, but they could commit a sin unknowingly.
When Iphis's father has done as he wishes,
It will be too late to tell him he cannot do it.

ERGASTE

That this business is already so far advanced

Could never have entered my mind.

TÉLÉTUZE

Ergaste, you must not argue with us.
Your sister and I know all this better than you.
What she has told you is the truth
And I am not the kind of woman to spread rumors.
But let us not indulge in such idle talk.
Are you of the same mind as you have ever been?

ERGASTE

What, to serve Iphis?

TÉLÉTUZE

To love our alliance;
To seek to fulfill it most anxiously.

ERGASTE

If the heavens are jealous of my noble resolve
And steal it from my heart, they will end my life.
Let hell prepare a new ordeal for me
If ever there is cause to call me unfaithful,
If ever I betray the innocent beauty
Who unknowingly holds my sweet freedom,
If I presume to look for more perfect charms
And if I am ungrateful for all you do for me!

TÉLÉTUZE

If you have ever thought of reaping the reward
Of your constant love, this is the time to act.
The conclusion of this impending marriage
Will ruin you and your future plans.
We must end this business.

ERGASTE

If I tell the secret, then,
You will not think me too indiscreet?

TÉLÉTUZE

In this extreme plight, I am willing to let it be known
And you should not fear to offend me.
Announce that you suffer from the torments of love
And reveal the object of your passion, but do it skillfully.

Act 2

Scene 1

ERGASTE *alone*

Who would not wonder at a love of this kind?
And who would fail to marvel at such an ardent flame?
I no longer know what to think of it and I cannot judge
If it should make me laugh or distress me further
When I see that a girl loves another like herself
And ignites her heart with a new kind of flame,
And that in this lovely couple, a garment only
Serves to distinguish between mistress and lover.
And although I can see that my goddess pines
For someone else, it only makes me laugh.
But I suffer also to see that, in fact,
A holy marriage will follow this buffoonish love affair.
The astonishing result of such an adventure
Drives me to despair and upsets nature.
I cannot allow such a dreadful day
To deprive me so shamefully of the fruit of my love.
Iphis, pleasant lover but cruel mistress,

You do not perceive how your gaze wounds me,
And you do not fully grasp what causes me to sigh,
You only hear my words as those of a friend;
You do not know me, and that is killing me,
And my sorrow arises only from having known you.
But to whom do you complain, poor Ergaste, and why
Are you angered that she pledges her love to another?
Since you see that she loves a girl rather than a man
Because of this newfound fire that consumes her,
You should at least find comfort in your suffering
To have a woman as a rival and not a man.
You know that to marry Iphis to Iante
Is to secure the fruit of your waiting
And that there is no surer way to preserve the honor
Of the precious object of your happiness.
But the dread of this feigned marriage
Makes me imagine a thousand reasons to fear.
I distrust every shadow and I start to suspect
That one of the two lovers might be a young man
And that the misfortune that keeps afflicting me,
With a second wonder, will lead to my utter ruin.
It is better, then, to reveal a secret
Than to repent later of having been too discreet.
To reveal her person, it is enough that I love her.
But how severe is my madness in this great endeavor,
Knowing that my love could disgrace her.
Alas! I love her so greatly that I dare not love her.

At least I hide it and everyone is unaware of
The wounds I receive from the eyes I adore.

Scene 2

Nise, Ergaste

NISE

Still dreaming all alone, deep in your worries?
It's the clever ones, really, who behave like that:
The conversation of these more rational souls
Is no match for their own fascinating thoughts.
But are you not at the wedding on the day that the gods
Give the young Iphis such a precious gift?

ERGASTE

I was on my way there.

NISE

How his heart rejoices
And how delighted he is to possess Iante!

ERGASTE

He has a right to be. If you had his success,
You would feel the same, perhaps with more excess.
When a suitor, by his own merits,
Has been raised above all honors,
When he is preferred among all his rivals,
Are these things, dear friend, cause for tears?

To possess both great wealth and a beautiful wife,
Is there a better way to ensure his own peace of mind?
Provided with such a match, how picky he would be
If he were not pleased with his great happiness?

NISE

Indeed, when one can find a favorable match,
Nothing is as pleasing as marriage.
Disparage it if you will, but I find there is nothing
That should be prized above this gift.
To live with a wife as well-behaved as beautiful
While a sacred bond unites us with her,
To enjoy the treasures that are rightfully ours,
To love and to be loved, is anything sweeter?
If we caress her, she also caresses us;
If we are her master, she is our mistress,
And all our happiness rests on this one point:
That our bodies and hearts are inseparable.
What a delight to see, without committing a vice,
The natural results of our chaste pleasures!
When Love, presiding over our embraces,
Brings forth the cause of our happiness,
And when, out of our beds, are produced
The little offshoots whose roots we are,
When we see them grow up and then, in our old age,
We seem to grow younger alongside our children.
This gentle yoke changes in our youth

Fury to reason and madness to wisdom,
And I find that Iphis acts quite prudently
To look after his happiness at an early age.
If I were permitted to be jealous of him,
I would wish myself the same happiness.
The thought of it alone delights my senses.
And you, what do you think?

ERGASTE

I agree with you.

NISE

How wonderful, Ergaste! And since your own voice
Confesses that this yoke is a great happiness
And that whoever finds it is most blessed,
Let me be the author of your felicity.
I have some influence over the mind of a young woman
Who can be considered a gentlewoman,
And if you consent to endorse my plans,
She can be yours.

ERGASTE

How very thoughtful of you.

NISE

What, would you not agree to marriage?

ERGASTE

I lack the courage for such a high endeavor.

NISE

Yet you approve of it.

ERGASTE

My own interests aside,
I want what you want; I like what you like.
Whatever your advice, I will follow it
So long as it is not contrary to my way of life.
But in the name of this beautiful friendship that joins us,
Do not do me any favors, since I do not ask for any.
Your goodwill strikes me as tyranny:
Against my natural inclination, you want me constrained.
You find my whim distasteful; my mood does not please you,
But bear with your friend, imperfect as he is,
Since it is in love that happiness resides
And that my inclination is to resist this god's laws.
In short, since to find happiness one must love first,
Allow me, all in good time, to fall in love.

NISE

And when will you resolve to burn with the fire
That sooner or later love ignites in all souls?
When will you resolve to allow your heart
To become a new throne for this young conqueror?
When would you like this sweet tyrant to reside in you,
And when will you love, if not this very moment?
If your heart does not vow to love from now on

And if it does not yet love, it will never love.
Do you want a prolonged sorrow in old age,
Blaming yourself for having so misused the privileges of youth?
Do you think thus to pervert the natural course of age
And to harvest in winter the flowers of your spring?
To become love's conquest, are you waiting
To burn when snow covers your head
And for your slow and weak body
To seek excitement when it cannot cope?
Do you think that this young Cupid who flees old age
Would ignite a heart in a frozen body
And that this delicate fire will invigorate an old body
When both time and wear have used it up?
You are wrong, Ergaste! You can be sure
That love does not reside in old ruins!
In a young heart, it is a heaven of pleasures,
Just as in an old mind, a hell of desires.
Love then, while you can.

ERGASTE

You see, Nise,
How I like your cleverness, your humor, your frankness.
You see that I love Iphis as much as one can love
The most divine object that can ever charm us,
And with all the virtues that fill his beautiful soul,
I think him preferable to the world's most beautiful women.

NISE

You speak of friendship, but I speak of love.

ERGASTE

To tell the truth, to this day my heart
Has not stooped to the disgraceful task
Of losing one's mind to win over a woman.
I prize their beauty, but among their charms
They have moods that I do not like.
I have an aversion for this flighty sex
Whose dull pursuit effeminates one's courage.

NISE

Is one less brave for it? You know well that in the past
Superb conquerors accepted its laws
And that beautiful eyes, using all their charms,
With a single glance made the most valiant of heroes
surrender arms, as the tales tell:
Was Achilles not a woman?[6] Did Hercules not spin thread?[7]
Hercules, who, to obey the wishes of a king,

6. According to a Greek legend, Achilles's mother knew that her son would die in the Trojan War. To avoid this fate, she dressed him as a girl and had him raised at the court of Lycomedes, king of Scyros, for many years. Of course, Achilles would eventually take part in the Trojan War and meet his fatal destiny.

7. Omphale, queen of Lydia, bought Hercules as a slave and required him to wear women's clothing and to spin wool. Numerous seventeenth- and eighteenth-century paintings, such as Peter Paul Rubens's *Hercules and Omphale* (c. 1602) and François Boucher's *Hercule et Omphale* (c. 1730), portray the legendary story.

Provided so much work for the scissors of Atropos?[8]
He who alone fought all the various monsters
And whose invincible strength cleansed the universe!
You profess to imitate on this earth
The actions of this formidable warrior:
He loved in his time; you should love in yours
And fully become Hercules, as he was.
Love one who adores you, Ergaste, and who urges you
To accept a match proposed by a friend.

ERGASTE

Is she beautiful?

NISE

She does not lack charm.

ERGASTE

Is she young?

NISE

Of the age to be loved.

ERGASTE

Is she rich?

8. One of the three goddesses of fate in Greek mythology, Atropos symbolizes death. Her sister Clotho spins the web of life, while her other sister Lachesis assigns the length of one's life. Finally, Atropos cuts the threads of life with her scissors.

NISE

Enough for your comfort.
She is quite perfect and leaves nothing to be desired.

ERGASTE

She is worth much, then.

NISE

She is a treasure.

ERGASTE

Believe me,
Since she is a treasure, keep her for yourself.
Yet, do not take this to be my last word.

NISE

Would you advise me to commit incest?
The one whose charms you should adore
Is too close to me for us to be joined:
I would marry my sister.

ERGASTE

Your sister?

NISE

She is the one
Who cherishes your virtue, who honors and loves you
With the most chaste and passionate love
A girl has ever shown for her lover.

She revealed the burning love that consumes her
And I knew the cause of it when she named you.
I would like to see my efforts procure her
What she can only hope from you alone, Ergaste.

ERGASTE

You are speaking in truth?

NISE

If you knew the sorrows
That Love makes her suffer in your sweet chains,
Unless your heart be most cruel, you would believe
That she makes herself ill in wishing you well.
The love she has for you deserves its reward;
She pays too dearly for her efforts to please you
For your sleepy mind not to be awakened.
Her adoring eyes are somewhat blinded by you.
If your heart's wishes were not opposed to mine,
We could henceforth from friends become brothers.
Much happiness would befall our houses
From such a union.

ERGASTE

And much honor to me:
You both do me a great favor
And I know well how unworthy I am of it.
Seeing nothing in me that is not a flaw,
To aspire to your sister's hand is to aim a bit high.

In any case, my wishes in such business
Depend entirely on those of a mother,
But I would count myself perfectly happy
If her approval authorized my wishes.
In the meantime, my soul will continue to languish,
Just like Iphis's.

NISE *seeing Iphis*

Here he comes from seeing Iante.

ERGASTE

Allow me to speak to him.

NISE

She comes also.

ERGASTE

Then let us leave them alone to speak
And not rob them of the pleasure of a few minutes.
I will accompany you to your home now
And return later, at a better time,
To have a word with him.

Scene 3

Iante, Iphis

IANTE

To be so secretive and to persist in not telling me
What dampens your usual gay spirit

And not reveal to me what weighs on your heart,
You are treating your lover with such cruelty.
When you promised before that all of your destiny
Would be shared with me and be ours equally,
When you gave me your heart, it was an empty promise.
Call me your queen as you did before,
But it is now a meaningless title
Since my hold on you is not absolute.
I never wanted to doubt it until now.

IPHIS

Alas! I die to hear you speak like this.
If you continue to have your doubts,
With these accusations your inhuman voice
Will cause my death and do cruelly
What one dart from your eyes does so sweetly.
At least, my dear life, you will not doubt
The exalted love that ravishes my soul,
And you may see before the day is done
How Iphis is for you a miracle of love.
You will see by the extreme pain that kills me
That one can love a divine thing too much
And you will accuse me, having received my pledge,
Of cherishing your beauty more than I should.

IANTE

You certainly do not flatter me with false praises
Or compliment my merits with those strange words
Commonly used by other lovers.

IPHIS

You will also learn that Iphis is unlike them.
If I do not mimic their foolish fire,
My heart unveils itself sincerely.
If I do not praise your charms enough,
My soul at least is not falsely disguised.

IANTE

Your frankness pleases me. I do not blame you
If my beauty is less than the blaze of your burning heart.
I know . . .

IPHIS

We ought not discuss it.
Your merit is great . . .

IANTE

But your love is greater?

IPHIS

You are not far off the mark.

IANTE

Your love would be quite small
If you compared it to my lack of merit.
It is enough that love compels us,
Though unequal in merit, to burn with the same fire.
You sigh. Tell me the secret that disturbs you.
How can you know something unless your heart knows it?
Is appearing sad today how you take delight
In the happiness that you so desired?
Have you recently seen a new face?
Are you not satisfied with our marriage?
Seeing that nothing can delay it now,
Is that what causes you to sigh?
By the sacred power of the god that ties us,
Let me know the reason for your melancholy.

IPHIS

It is true. I sigh.

IANTE

Yes?

IPHIS

To see myself
Unworthy of the honor I will receive.
A thousand suitors drawn by the light of your grace
Contested this prize and the least of them has won it.

Love kindled so many perfect rivals against me
And I vanquished them, with all my shortcomings.

IANTE

Does it upset you?

IPHIS

You know it does, my soul,
And you can be sure of it since you know how I burn.
You know that my heart should be troubled
Like one that was dying and has been healed.
I regret only that this pleasant marriage,
Which brings me happiness, will bring you misery
And that, in uniting us under the same law,
This bond which is held so dear will be so only for me.
I know my own weakness and I feel guilty
To accept a treasure for which I am unfit;
And, to speak honestly, I do not deserve,
Imperfect as I am, such perfect charms.

IANTE

You seek your own defeat with these diversions,
But you are imperfect only in judging me perfect.
And since I have made you the object of my love,
Should you be lesser than me, I would still love you.
If heaven, in marrying us, wants me to be deceived,
What of it? You will have happily tricked me.
And if at last this makes me unhappy,

If it is for you, I will not complain.
Both our hearts were afflicted with the same wound
And not to love each other is to go against nature.
Your person charms me and I am not worried
That, with you, what is inside could fool what is outside.
But I say too much and I do not take heed
That in these words said freely my honor is at stake.
Also, time is passing, and while we are speaking,
Your father and mine are not concluding the contract.

IPHIS

I will go and find him; I die of impatience.
But first, a kiss.

IANTE

Have two in advance.

Scene 4

Ergaste, Iante, Iphis

ERGASTE *seeing them kiss*

What a good prospect he[9] has chosen to marry off his sister;
As if I wanted her to be mine!
But here is our lover kissing his mistress:
She receives from him a last embrace.
Tonight promises her much better amusement,
But all that she hopes for, she will not find.

9. Here, Ergaste refers to Nise.

IANTE

Return with your father in no more than an hour.

IPHIS

My burning desire cannot allow a long wait.

Scene 5

Ergaste, Iphis

ERGASTE *approaching Iphis*

And so, my dear Iphis, after all your sighing
This auspicious day will crown your love?
Are you given today the marvel of all beauties?
I am truly delighted to hear this good news.
I knew, as one of your dear confidants,
That she was the object of your burning desire,
That your illness was too violent
To be healed lest you married Iante.
I knew that your wishes all tended to that end,
But I did not think it would happen so soon
And I can scarcely believe it
Unless you yourself give me your assurance.
So then, will you marry her?

IPHIS

Fate wants it so.

ERGASTE

And you?

IPHIS

It is what I desire.

ERGASTE

I thought as much.

IPHIS

Her beauty delights me.

ERGASTE

Really, being so beautiful,

She truly deserves to have Iphis burn for her.

IPHIS

Do not mock me! But tell me if you have ever seen

Anything remotely approaching her charms.

ERGASTE *sighing*

I see you everyday.

IPHIS

But tell me if your heart,

Like mine, has felt the amorous flame?

Or rather, tell me: If the one who has charmed my heart

Loved you as much or more than she loves me,

If her eagerness to become your beloved

Revealed to your eyes her pressing desire,
Tell me without fearing my jealousy,
How much would you love her?

ERGASTE

I promise, less than you.

IPHIS

What! You would not love the one that I revere
With boundless love? Your heart says otherwise.
This sigh betrays you, else I would think you
Wilder than a tiger and less of a man than I.

ERGASTE

I say only that my love would be more passionate
For the gentle Iphis than for the beautiful Iante.

IPHIS

Say rather your friendship.

ERGASTE

I always get confused
With these distinctions between love and friendship.
In any case, my heart would desire above all else
That the gods cause in you a metamorphosis
So that I could love you differently.
You really are too beautiful for a man.
Nature, who delighted in making you adorable,

Should have made you a girl or less lovable,
And having given you the means to inflict death,
She should also have given you the means to heal:
I would have burned for you with a more legitimate fire
And my heart would then have been your victim.
At the risk of arousing heaven's anger,
I would have known no goddess but you.
But would you have loved me?

IPHIS

How frivolous these thoughts are
And what a waste of time and words!
Let us talk sensibly. Have I found a good match?

ERGASTE

We will never see a couple better matched:
Is it not right, Iante being such a beauty,
That an accomplished lover like Iphis be for her?
How happy you will be together and how the days,
The weeks, the months, the years will seem short!
I will not wish on your wedding night
for your desire to engender a successful lineage.
Heaven will grant these perfect treasures
To your embraces, rather than my wishes.
And since when you speak you deliver oracles,
By having children you will make miracles.
Farewell, then, I leave you at the mercy of Love.

Sleep heartily while the day lasts:
This night which favors the fire that consumes you
Will be for labor rather than for sleep.

Scene 6

IPHIS *alone*

This joker's taunts put me on edge.
He has reason to laugh at my expense.
My suspicious mind is in doubt:
His sister is my mother's confidante;
She knows our secrets and thus through her
I fear that this trickster knows me only too well.
I speak to him as a friend but the friend harasses me
Like a lovestruck suitor would harass his beloved.
He sighs before my eyes and remains dumbfounded
Just like a lover flustered by his shame.
The strongest of friendships does not drive a man
To this sort of exuberance with such audacity;
And, as I see it, my soul holds the same power
Over him as Iante has over me.
What strange effects of love! I pine for this beauty
And yet, alas, I am a girl, like her!
I love her charms, which are beyond compare.
I am a girl; she is too, and I must marry her!
Oh, pitiful Iphis! Unfortunate Iante!
Which of us two will consummate our marriage?

What! I would hold this charming treasure in my arms,
I would possess it but not take pleasure from it?
I would hold the object of my soul's devotion
And make such poor use of the favors obtained?
What! The heavens, without quenching my fire,
Would turn me from blissful suitor to unhappy possessor?
What! I would fall asleep next to this beauty
And would not do the impossible for her?
I would be useless in such a worthy cause?
No, the good goddess will take pity on me.

Act 3

Scene 1

Mérinte, Nise

MÉRINTE

In a word, tell me whether I am to live or die.
Do not prolong my anguish; satisfy my desire;
Prevent my ruin or let me perish.
Be sweet to me or cruel; give me life or death;
Tell me if your appeal has touched his heart,
If he was swayed.

NISE

What more would you like?
Have I not told you everything?

MÉRINTE

You were only flattering me
With the tales you have just told me.
To say that my love is the source of his joy
Is saying a bit too much to be believable.

You failed to sway his heart, so you wish to conceal
And sweeten the poison that I must ingest.

NISE

Let me die if I am lying or hiding something.
You really are being too incredulous.

MÉRINTE

Treat me less severely, I beg of you,
And unburden your heart of all that you know.
When at last I learn from you that his cruel heart despises
The sincere gift that my heart offers him,
That my sighs are in vain, that they have no power,
And that like a mountain he cannot be moved
And has a heart that rebels against love and pity,
You will only tell me what I already know.
And when you tell me that he rejects my pledge,
Alas! My despair told me so before you
And I was not expecting a more favorable fate.

NISE

You and your love are becoming bothersome.

MÉRINTE

I become bothersome? The cruel man complains of it?
His eyes continuously make me suffer.
I find pleasure in being unhappy

At having made him the object of my burning desire.
I love him, adore him, and that inhuman man
Mocks my desires; my love offends him.
I have until now silenced my grief:
I chose to stifle it despite its violence.
And the first time that he hears of me,
He calls me bothersome and rejects my pledge.
This handsome tyrant wounds us yet does not want
Those who feel his blows to complain.
Well then, I must die and no longer be a bother
To this untamable heart who renders my desires useless.
He would be quite cruel if, when I breathe my last,
He does not allow me to speak of my burning love.
And his scorn for me would be great
If, as I die, he finds my last breath bothersome.

NISE

I think your love will finally make you mad;
While you should be laughing, we have to console you.
I alone complain of the inconvenience
And of having a sister always at my side.
I have told you a hundred times; I will say it again:
He cherishes you as much as your heart loves him.

MÉRINTE

Alas! If it were true, I would have such happiness!

NISE

Your love delights him and honors him greatly.
If your heart seemed to him a worthless conquest,
Could he not find some decent excuse
And reject your advances with a polite statement,
Forcing you to seek another lover elsewhere?
He could have declared that he did not wish
Ever to be ensnared by a beautiful face.

MÉRINTE

He is too well versed in the art of pleasing at court
To openly declare his refusal of my love.
He is too much a courtier to say frankly
That he wants nothing to do with someone he despises.
Even if, in his eyes, I possessed no charms
And he could not love me, he would not say it.
Disdain on his lips would appear unrefined.
One must yell fire when one is cold as ice,
Flatter the one who loves us and make the effort,
At least, to put on a brave face.
It is no more effort to pretend that we love
Than to make a display of extreme rigor,
And the inclination for acts easily performed
Compels a gracious man to act with civility.
All his promises are nothing but courtesy.
He may have a hundred mistresses and still be free.
His fire lasts no more than his conversation,

And the divine object who enchants me so
Is one of those people who have learned in wicked circles
To heal hearts but only with words.

NISE

Hearing you speak so thoughtfully, it seems
You owe your misfortune to your own reasoning.
Your doubting mind, with its suspicions,
Would be more at rest had it less caution.
For what reason would he not love you?
Your face is not so devoid of charm.
Were you to become his wife, this marriage
Would not be so unfavorable to him.
On what do you base your suspicions of his scorn?
Do you think him smitten by another?

MÉRINTE

Dear brother, there you touch upon the cause of my fear.

NISE

Is that all the worry that afflicts your soul?
His heart knows neither love nor its flame.

MÉRINTE

But, dear brother, he is a man; he is young; he is beautiful.
It is quite strange that with such attributes
He has not yet won the heart of a beloved
And that a fortunate lady has not yet conquered his.

NISE

If he has exchanged his heart, it is with yours
And it is you only that he wants for a wife.

MÉRINTE

I have no rival and yet I am jealous;
I am possessed by a fury that rules over me.

NISE

Be jealous only of Iphis or of me.
Though your burning love may have warmed his cold heart,
We are both well ahead in his good graces.
And you can be assured that if he is not in love,
If he does not love you, his love is only for the two of us.
His friendship is well worth the most extreme love.
But here he comes.

MÉRINTE

Dear brother, it is he.

NISE

Tame your passion and hide your feelings.

MÉRINTE

Oh gods! How difficult it will be to contain my fire!

Scene 2

Ergaste, Nise, Mérinte

ERGASTE *thinking that he is alone*

My mind is being kept in suspense too long.
Secrets that are silenced hold too much violence.

NISE *surprising him*

That is true, so why not share with us a secret
That your heart can only hide reluctantly?

ERGASTE

I tire at last to see trickery
And disguise rule in my country;
And I wish, out of pity, to enlighten the minds
That have been fooled in vain by ruse and error.

MÉRINTE *to herself*

Cruel man! If my love had filled your soul,
Alas, how sweetly you would have enlightened me!

NISE

Your muddled words make me curious.
You make no sense; explain yourself better.

ERGASTE

My friend, you will know everything, but let us go to
  Téleste's
Where I have resolved to inform you of the rest.

His daughter is marrying Iphis, and there you will see
The outcome of the words which do not fully satisfy you.

NISE

Let us go. I can see that my sister ventures
To follow us; I place her in your care.

ERGASTE

You do me an honor to which I was not aspiring.

NISE

Walk ahead anyway; I follow in your footsteps.
[to himself]
Loving compliments should be forthcoming.
How badly he begins his offer of service.
He does not speak to her. I think that, after all
An overwhelming love chokes his voice.
He is about to start, but Iante has come out.
This cold suitor will have to postpone his effort.

Scene 3

Iante, Ergaste, Nise, Mérinte

IANTE *coming to greet them*

You come just in time. We were waiting for you
To make official what is being done here.

ERGASTE

Were we not to witness these new nuptials,
This event in itself is solemn enough.
It is too uncommon and this new treaty
Is much too unusual to be kept a secret.
But what happiness must pervade in your soul!
To be the wife of such a perfect husband!
What a charming man is the loving Iphis!
What a brave spouse, what a beautiful lover!
Whatever good looks he offers your beautiful eyes,
You will see that, in fact, he is quite something else,
And while others may be better built, you will say today
That the most accomplished is not made quite like him.

NISE

We cannot equal him, just as we are.
In him, madam marries the marvel of all men.

MÉRINTE

He alone is worthy of possessing her heart.
She must really love him.

IANTE

Indeed, I love him, dear sister.

ERGASTE *laughing*

I love him as much as you do.

IANTE

On that score,
No jealousy can trouble my imagination.

ERGASTE

And how would you feel toward my plight
If I were your rival for the love of Iphis?
I will not keep you in doubt any longer:
Know that Iphis is a girl and that I pine for her.

IANTE

Ha! What amusing words!

ERGASTE

You think that I jest
And that my voice tricks you, rather than Iphis's clothing?

IANTE

Truly, Ergaste's mood and his lovely obsession
Will soon make this entire gathering laugh.

Scene 4

Téleste, Ligde, Iante, Ergaste, Nise, Mérinte

TÉLESTE *to Ligde*

I have already told you that it was my intent,
That it is best to do it today rather than tomorrow.
And so, if you agree, by the end of the day,
The contract for such a lovely marriage will be concluded.

LIGDE

I have come to see you especially.

TÉLESTE

Then let Iphis marry my daughter who stands here.
Are you in agreement with us?

LIGDE

I have already said that he would have no other.

TÉLESTE

Why did you not bring him along and your wife as well?

LIGDE

Both mother and son will be here shortly.
When our children are under the laws of marriage,
Let the heavens ever bless their house.
Let the gentlest stars, and the least harsh,
Shine unceasingly upon this loving couple.
Let happiness never fade from their house
And let their innocent bed bear good fruit.

ERGASTE

What support you will have for the end of your days
And how wrong I am if they do not have beautiful children!

TÉLESTE

Let the heavens be favorable to Téleste's wishes
And keep away from their lives any dreadful event;

And let them richly bestow upon their family
The favors whose graces enrich human life.

NISE

Keep them from harm at all stages of life.
Let no quarrel trouble their household.
Let peace reign in their house, keep them far from troubles,
And may their days be as delightful as their nights.

MÉRINTE

What new wishes can this lovely couple hope for?
You have said so much that I can do no more
And I would not know what else to wish for them
Other than to see all you have said come true.

ERGASTE

Let the heavens, who know the deepest secrets,
Open your eyes to let you see what you are doing.
Therein lies all my heart's desire.
A sin of ignorance remains a sin.
In this fatal venture where hell is leading you,
You will perform a crime rather than a marriage.
Nature and love oppose all your efforts.

TÉLESTE

Who would prevent us from concluding our agreement?

ERGASTE

It is enough that they cannot be married.

TÉLESTE

I think he is mad, Ligde. What do you think?

IANTE

You must seek elsewhere a better match for me;
Someone Ergaste will think better suited.

TÉLESTE

Ergaste, what business of yours is my family?
Do you rule my daughter's mind absolutely?
Have you decided to govern my old age?
Has heaven made you the father of my children?
My daughter belongs to me; what rights do you have?
Had I promised you that you would be my son-in-law?
Do you want to take her and deprive me of the power
Granted to me as a father to provide for her?

ERGASTE

That is not my intent.

TÉLESTE

You could not do so.

IANTE

You have no reason to become angry.
When you learn of the affliction from which Ergaste suffers,

You will regret at once having become upset.
I am not the object that tickles his fancy,
But it is rather the one whose wife I must be.
His deranged fire burns for Iphis only.

LIGDE

Well, that is a good story!

TÉLESTE

I was quite surprised.

MÉRINTE

My dear brother, I am getting worried by this game.

NISE

It has gone on too long to be only a pretense.

LIGDE

So then, Ergaste is in love with Iphis.
He wants to be my son-in-law, and yet a son is all I have!

ERGASTE

How blind nature is! A father who does not know
His own progeny ceases to be one, really.
Act with maturity in this matter.
Consider that Iphis is a girl and Iante also.
By the sacred respect due to marriage,
Which both are abusing to their own disadvantage,

By Iphis's beautiful eyes, which have ravished my heart,
Do not pursue this course.

LIGDE

He is in a fine mood.

TÉLESTE

No doubt, after consulting with his bottles,
We can be assured that he will prophesize marvels.

IANTE

His words strike with such sincerity
That to hear them one would think them true.

MÉRINTE

It is in vain that I yearn for the torment that possesses me.

NISE

Ergaste, the time is past to mock us this way.
We must know the design that you keep in your heart.
Are you doing this for laughs or do you intend
To break your agreement to a certain marriage
For which you have given your word?
You must ratify in front of all our friends
What we have promised each other secretly
And publicly declare your heart's resolve
Regarding your choice of a wife.

ERGASTE

In short, know that I love Iphis,
That I die for her, that I live for her,
That Love and fate have made me for her,
And that even in death, I will be faithful to her.

MÉRINTE

Traitor! So now you are being a joker,
Mocking my brother and laughing at his sister?
My burning desire must drown with my tears
And your words must hurt me, as much as your charms.
You want me to increase my shame and my sorrow
By revealing my love and showing my weakness.
Yes, I have loved this ungrateful man and am not ashamed
To say that he is the one with whom I fell in love.
He was the first temple to receive my burning offerings
And will be the last altar to receive my prayers.

ERGASTE

For a long time, Lady, another beauty has held me.
Would you think kindly of a treacherous, flighty man?
You could not love me after such an insult.
But if I had two hearts, you would have the second.

MÉRINTE

One would be quite foolish to believe you
Since another than I reigns in your mind.
Go, deceiver, perjurer! Go adore her charms!

IANTE

What, you loved him, Mérinte, and said nothing?

NISE

Nor did you, Ergaste, whom I name unworthy.

ERGASTE

If you feel offended, you really know your man.

NISE

Truly, you could not speak more to the point.
An hour from now, we will have words.

TÉLESTE

Do not quarrel, but let us spend the day
Enjoying the happiness provided by this marriage.
Besides, in all decency, you must not shirk
From signing the contract that we will ratify.

ERGASTE

What! Let my signature approve such an injustice?
Heaven keep me from being party to it.
Instead, I will go this instant and split open my veins
And, with my blood sign my own death warrant.
You incredulous old men! Respect for your age
Is what allows me to forgive such a grave insult.
I would otherwise shorten your lengthy days.

LIGDE

Let us go in. He has completely lost his senses.

Scene 5

ERGASTE *now alone*

Yes, in losing my beloved, I have lost my senses.
My mind is completely overcome by this oppressive burden,
And at the bitter end of my cruel torment,
It would be senseless to be reasonable.
Since I am losing Iphis and she is taken from me,
All that is left for me is to end my life.

Act 4

Scene 1

Iphis, Iante, in a bedroom

IPHIS

Do not force me to reveal this to you.
My love, allow me to die without having to speak.
I can neither hide from you nor dare tell you
The important matter which compels me to sigh.
I love you. Allow me to die
So that after my death, you will know the rest.
Accept this compelling proof of my burning love.
You are my wife; you will be my widow.
Alas! It is for this fate that we are united.
My desire and your woes will become boundless.

IANTE

Your complaint is now pointless and superfluous
Since you can see that the deal is done,
Since marriage is a Gordian knot,[10]

10. From an ancient Greek legend, refers to a knot that cannot be untied.

Since only death can sever this bond,
And, since until now, you have chosen to pretend,
It is time to suffer, rather than to complain.
If you had no intent to give me your faith,
If you did so only to laugh at my expense,
If your soul was falsely inflamed,
Intending only to see me deceived
So that you could better taunt the object of your scorn,
You should have been careful not to get trapped yourself.
If we are united in this intimate bond,
It is because of your misfortune or your carelessness.
You feigned to love me and, with that convincing front,
I felt for you a fierce love.
When your contrived words delighted my ears,
I should simply have done the same to you.
Instead, I decided to give myself entirely,
Trading a true love with one that was false.
But I would have sworn that, far from deceiving me,
You also felt the torment that gnawed at my soul,
And in your desire to see yourself as my husband,
You pined for me as I do for you.
But having given yourself to me, your sorrow is a sign
That you judge me unworthy of such a fine gift.
Given the predicament we face, the two of us,
My only misfortune is to see you unhappy
And I would almost want you to take back a heart
That I could not give you back without my own.

IPHIS

What! Do you doubt that Iphis adores your charms?
Ha! If you loved me truly, you would not doubt it.
Allow me to banish this unwelcome concern
By showing you my heart; you will see how it burns.
Let me tear it out with my own hands, right now,
And you will know who loves you and I will die happy.
You will learn a secret difficult to understand.
Your eyes will see a heart they have reduced to ashes,
A heart that your gaze has already consumed,
That could have loved you more had it loved you less,
A heart that nature made contrary to others
And that alone is the cause of your woes and mine.

IANTE

I believe you are crying.

IPHIS

My dear heart, with these tears
Learn the cause of my legitimate woes.
Let my eyes reveal what my lips cannot.
They can expose the worry that afflicts me.
In my predicament, to say that I love you
And kiss this beautiful breast is all that I can do.
O gods! Will you leave me to die of thirst
Next to a fountain, to add to my suffering?[11]

11. This metaphor is commonly used in French medieval poetry by authors such as François Villon and Charles d'Orléans.

Will I see before me such delicate morsels
And when they are served, will I not taste them?
Am I to hold in my arms the fairest beauty in the world
And next to her, be like Tantalus in the pool?[12]
Alas! My dear half (since I am your husband,
You become so), how I suffer for you.

IANTE

I suffer even more from not knowing
The cause that drives you to such anxiety,
And the desire to know what ails you
Torments my heart with incomparable angst.
Tell me this secret and any others you have;
They are my business, since they belong to you.
If the matter affects you, then it does me also
And my soul must take its share of the worry.
Who then is making you so sad and withdrawn?
Iphis, is it with me that you must remain silent?
I am your half. Therefore, your heart in this case
Can only know half of something I do not know.
Reveal a secret to the one who loves you;
To divulge it to me is to divulge it to yourself,
And I love you too much not to take part
In the sad event that is afflicting you.

---

12. Tantalus was punished by the gods for attempting to appear as their equal during a banquet he offered them. As a punishment, they displayed objects he desired within his reach but that remained elusive. Tantalus thus symbolizes unfulfilled desire.

IPHIS

Alas! Can you not read in my mind
The strange movement of my irrational fire?
Can my heart explain it any better than with sighs?
And can you not see in my eyes the suffering that grips me?
We are married and this auspicious night
Delivers to my wishes an adorable treasure.
Our elated parents leave us in this place
So as not to interrupt a divine mystery.
Marriage, which converts crime into innocence,
Gives my young desires every license.
I am in love. I possess you. In my delaying
Do you not suspect my secret torment?
I say too much and want the fatal moment
That will bring me death to teach you the rest.
Dark sister of sleep, end my sorrows
Or else let me become what they think that I am.

Scene 2

Ergaste, Téleste's servant[13]

ERGASTE

Is everything concluded?

13. The original text neglects to mention this character at the beginning of the scene.

SERVANT

I believe that it is.
As we speak, they are lying together.

ERGASTE

Already? So early! Such a fierce fire
Could not let them wait much longer.
How did this pleasant marriage end?
Is everyone quite happy?

SERVANT

None could be happier.
I think everyone thanks their fate.
If they were solemn at the wedding, they will laugh at the feast!

ERGASTE

Tell me how the business ended
And how the parents concluded the marriage.

SERVANT

They all assembled at Téleste's, and first,
As they wished, they finalized the agreement.
Everyone present bore witness
That they also approved this new marriage
And the fathers looked twenty years younger.

ERGASTE

And the newlyweds, were they quite happy?

SERVANT

Yes, but I reckon, in his heart, the husband
Was not as pleased as his new wife:
His mind seemed troubled.
He should have been happier, but did not seem so.
And when it was time, as is customary,
For him to consent by taking up the pen,
A sigh escaped him and made me see finally
That he was signing his name reluctantly.
I do not wish to read a bad omen into it.
They are people, it seems to me, that can get along well.
His heart, impatient to see the end of the day,
May have sighed out of love.

ERGASTE

And was Iphis's mother there also
When the matter was coming to a close?

SERVANT

They thought they would never get her to consent.
She threatened that they would quickly regret it,
Claiming that the gods were not favorable
Toward this marriage, which was a mismatch,
And that the greatest of misfortunes
Would follow this wedding.

ERGASTE

But did she sign?

SERVANT

Ligde threatened her, so she did by force
What should have been done freely as a holy gesture.
She could not hold back and protested
That she was signing against her will.

Scene 3

ERGASTE

Go! I know more than I need. Ha! Heavens, how is it
That I still have feelings and that I am not dead!
I suffer from a wound that should have killed me
And must be immortal since I do not die.
O unyielding death! Have I long to live
This violent despair that destiny sends me?
O Love! Who relishes in treating me so badly!
Return my mistress to me or grant me a rival.
Take pity. Listen to my plea!
One of the two enchants me, or at least consoles me.
If you wish to heal me from such painful torment,
Let her be in fact what she pretends to be
And let the change of her unfaithful sex
Also change the love that I feel for her.
But can I ask mercy from such a false enemy?
Can I expect any good from the author of my woes?
The gods are against me. Everything tends to my ruin.
Love breaks its own rules in order to harm me

And, in its cruelty, is so set against my wishes
That it commits a crime to see me unhappy.

Scene 4

Nise, Ergaste

NISE

My plan has won over all their mistrust:
I have escaped despite the vigilance
Of these Arguses[14] who were looking out for my departure.
But I fear that I may have come too late
Or that this traitor has left by a different route.
I think he is coming. I wonder,
Is he passing by or waiting for me?
Ergaste!

ERGASTE

Eh! Dear friend! Who knew you were so near?

NISE

Were you not waiting for me, at the hour appointed
By the summons you have given me?

ERGASTE

Me?

14. In Greek mythology Argus was a giant prince with a hundred eyes on his body. Fifty of his eyes remained constantly open to watch over Io, Zeus's lover, of whom Hera, Zeus's wife, was jealous.

NISE

Words are useless here.

ERGASTE

I swear by my faith that it had escaped my mind.

NISE

This is how this true and open heart,
This honest disposition, this accommodating man,
Forgetting what he has promised,
Takes pride in discarding his friends.
Let us get on with it.

ERGASTE

If you think that I have offended you,
It would not be right to defend myself.
Although I still doubt that I am guilty,
Punish me, avenge yourself, I will consider myself as such.

NISE

What! Do you still not know the nature
Of a traitor or what name must be given to his actions?
You well deserve a double punishment
For one sins twice by calling one's fault praiseworthy.
To mock a friend, to break your word,
Are these vain and frivolous actions?

ERGASTE

But Iphis's beauty triumphs over my word.

NISE

Enough games. Defend yourself or die.

ERGASTE

Since it is night and we are near this door,
With all the noise we will make, I fear someone will come out
And that your anger against a friend
May only be satisfied in part.
Let us wait until tomorrow.

NISE

Your heart is made of ice.
One of us must remain on this spot.
The sun does not wish to shine upon us and
Honor the death of a deceitful man such as you.
They fight.

Scene 5

Mérinte, Ligde, Téleste, Ergaste, Nise

MÉRINTE

Hurry! I hear some noise.

LIGDE

How unfortunate!
We should have remembered that they had quarreled.

TÉLESTE

Who would have been wary of his sudden departure?

LIGDE

They are quite stirred up to fight at this late hour.

ERGASTE

Well, at least I am defending myself.

MÉRINTE *between them*

Help! Murder!
Oh, dear brother! Ah, deceitful man! I exert myself in vain!

ERGASTE

Lady, you think me the aggressor.

MÉRINTE

Traitor! Spare my brother and take his sister's life.

TÉLESTE

Let us get a little closer: I hear Mérinte shouting.
I fear that in this commotion, she may have been wounded.
What enrages you so, children? What is this?
Must two friends be at each other's throats like this?
That should be enough for you. Put away your swords:
Let them be used for much greater deeds.
You are acting like such foolish knaves,
Fighting for no reason. Are you hurt?
That is all I fear.

ERGASTE

Your fear is well founded.
Alas, I suffer from an incurable wound!

LIGDE

O gods! Is it possible? Oh, unfortunate plan!
Go quickly and fetch the physician.

MÉRINTE

Is this traitor wounded? Let us be helpful;
One must be charitable to one's enemies.

ERGASTE

Marvel of all beauties, you should better employ the cares
With which your charity seeks to help me.
And you, wise elders, whose old-fashioned wisdom
Brings futile relief to the torment that stings me,
Do not exert yourselves in trying to heal me.
Since I cannot live and since I wish to die,
Your help is in vain for the ill that afflicts me.
My wound is to the heart and Iphis is my cure.

MÉRINTE

It is easy to judge from his words
That he is never content lest he be deceiving.

LIGDE

The blow is not fatal.

TÉLESTE

What a strange obsession!
His poor mind suffers in endless sorrow.
We must satisfy him by some device.
Ergaste, do you agree to the following condition?

ERGASTE

Which one?

TÉLESTE

Should it be that the object of the fire that
consumes you
Does not possess the perfections that make a man
And all that a woman demands of a husband,
We give you our pledge: you can have Iphis.
My daughter would not be displeased nor receive blame
Since, Iphis being a girl, she is not her wife.
But if that is not so, you must promise us
That you will marry Mérinte, who stands here.

ERGASTE

Agreed. I wish to make it a sacred promise,
Being only too happy in that case to have her as my beloved.

NISE

And if that is so, I want henceforth
That we two be friends again, as before.
It is the only way to put our quarrel to rest.

LIGDE

Early tomorrow, the bride will bring us news
And if her voice does not say that Iphis is a man,
There is another way for us to find out.

ERGASTE

I expected no better. How my soul is delighted!
Such charming words bring me back to life
And extreme pleasure occupies all my senses
As tomorrow we will see whose eyes are to be opened!
Finally, fate smiles upon me and love caresses me;
I keep a friend without losing a beloved.
Farewell, I have reached the goal that I desired.

TÉLESTE

What strange words! We will have the pleasure
To see into the haze that fills his mind
And how far his excessive madness will go.
If tomorrow Iphis does not set him right,
He can be certain this madness will last a long time.

Act 5

Scene 1

IANTE *alone*

Gods! Who would have suspected this! How this trickery
Is skillful at deceiving itself!
Who in the world has ever seen such a wonder?
For me, I believe it to be the effects of sleep.
And in the uncertainty in which my mind is thrown,
Such an event seems like a dream to me.
What a sad night, that lasted so long!
What great secrets you have revealed to me!
What circumstance can be like ours?
A girl, dear gods, marrying another!
We are sure to attract heaven's anger
And to become the talk of the theaters.
Such an encounter is worthy of being staged.
The fear of it afflicts me, I must confess.
This marriage is sweet, I find it attractive enough
And if people did not laugh, I would not complain.
I would not have any regrets in being joined together

If the knot that binds us was not being desecrated
And if our good parents did not freely misuse
This union that is held so sacred and holy.
If a girl married another like her
Without offending heaven and natural law,
My heart would certainly not be upset;
It would suffice me not to have sinned.
But since nature and heaven itself ordain
That a girl's pledge be given to a man
And that it is a man only that can receive it,
Iphis not being one, that is the source of all my troubles.
But what a frustrating battle I will face
With those who are happy with my fate
And who, judging only appearances,
Do not know at all what I feel in my heart.

Scene 2

Ligde, Téleste, Iante

LIGDE

Up so early after your wedding night?
This hour is for beauties in their widowhood.
You should have prolonged such a sweet night
To enjoy more thoroughly all that it offers.
It is true that these delights can be had any time
And that Hymen[15] receives offerings at all times.

15. Hymen is the god of marriage in Greek mythology.

Cupid, joined with this god, becomes all solemn
And is no longer hidden, no longer criminal.
He dims, and reveals a flame that is lit
Where before it dared not even show smoke.
He likes brightness. The day appears beautiful to him,
And, no longer ashamed, he no longer wears a blindfold;
It is no longer a sin, no longer an offense:
A sacred marriage grants complete freedom.

TÉLESTE

But you do not mention that love's sweet stolen
moments,
Wishing to remain secret, are enemies of the day.

LIGDE

Your daughter is blushing and her modest disposition
Recognizes its own thoughts in Téleste's words.

TÉLESTE

My daughter, you must suffer these little quips
And not lower your gaze in shame.
Do not get upset; this is customary.
He speaks to you as once was done to your mother.
And since you are not born of a better house,
Endure it, as she did, on such an occasion.
And also, you must, if you can,
Not be ungrateful for the happiness that favors you.
Your good fortune is flawless,

Your contentment has all it requires;
Your wishes are realized. You are quite happy.
You have a husband who meets your expectations:
Young, rich, well built.

LIGDE

You mock him.

TÉLESTE

He is your support, your aid, your comfort.
You love him; he loves you and he pines for you.
In a word, you have what your heart desires
And you are so happy in this perfection
That there are no wishes left for you to utter.
Heaven awards you favors it gives no other.
You could at least thank the hand that grants them.
Love your fate and follow its path
But be not blinded by the blindness of others.[16]
Your happiness is great; none can fully grasp it
But the hand that gave it can also take it away.
Your spouse is a gift that can be taken from you,
Costing as many tears as you shed to find him.
The gods have taken others, as beautiful as yours.
They give with one hand, take back with the other

16. The word *fate* and the idea of blindness evoke the Roman goddess Fortuna and the unpredictability of one's lot.

And their favors, whatever one has,
Benefit an ingrate only to better punish him.
Show some gratitude for their kindness
And make good use of this advice.

IANTE
Whether the gods be kind to me or harsh,
My soul has good reason to offer them prayers.
That is what leads me to the temple.

LIGDE
Your devotion will lead us by example
And we will follow you. We have a mind,
Your father and I, to lend you a hand.

Scene 3

IPHIS *alone*
At last, you must consent to your ruin:
Your sex is known; your shame uncovered.
Miserable toy of heaven and mortals,
There is . . . there is no time to embrace the altars.
What have I not deserved? I caused the unhappiness
Of the beauty who never showed me any harshness.
I have betrayed her and played a cowardly trick
Upon the one who sought to repay my love.
I make her miserable and my treacherous soul

Impudently takes advantage[17] of her beautiful youth.
Alas! I have done more than I can tell
Hoping for a pleasure I could not taste.
Oh the memory! But what? Could I have expected
To enjoy such pleasure, even if I could?
I, who have never seen any change in the wretched course
Of the ill-fated star that ordains my life?
I, who should have died rather than be born
Since it was the fate for which I was destined,
Since the gods wanted a mere moment
To distinguish between my beginning and my end,
And since even the author of my tragic life
Ordered it to be taken upon my birth.
My mother gave me useless clothing
And, had he known me, Iphis would be no longer.
My sex would have stifled his paternal love;
My sex, which already made me criminal.
I would have been happy to see Atropos end my days
The unfortunate moment they began!
I would not have had the honor to burn for Iante,
But, had I been dead, she would have been happy.

---

17. Here, the French version uses the term *abuser* ("to trick"). But the term also refers to the danger of the phallic figure of the lesbian in the social and medical discourses of the time. For instance, in *Traité des Hermaphrodites* (Paris, 1612), Jacques Duval writes, "[L]es femmes qui en sont bien munies en peuvent abuser les filles, leur donnant telle délectation que ferait un homme" ("[T]he women who are well-endowed can abuse girls, giving them the same pleasure as a man"; 68; our trans.). The term *abuser* reflects a fear of the lesbian's phallic potential.

I would not have been the cause of her tears:
She would be happy, and I, without misfortune.
I must seek death. How could I still live
Having cheated the beautiful eyes that I adore?
But who is it that saved me from the harsh punishment
I should have endured before I could sin?
Who has until now delayed the ordained punishment
To which I had been condemned before I was born?
It is not destiny, for fortune and fate
Are too much my enemies to be against my death.
Nor is it my father: he begged the one who gave birth to me
For me not to be, even before I was.
Who will you blame? Who is responsible for your life?
Who is the cause of this offense against you, oh miserable
Iphis!

Scene 4

Iphis, Télétuze

IPHIS *seeing her mother*

Oh, it is you!

TÉLÉTUZE

What have I done?

IPHIS

Whose cruel pity,
Rather than kill me, made me immortal.

To let me live like this, that was a betrayal.
You loved me so much; you should have hated me.
I would not have become fate's trophy
Had you suffocated me while you embraced me.
With your pity, you have made it plain to me
That you did not love me exceedingly.
To please the author of my existence, you should have
Prevented me from being a girl or from being born.
You would not have done wrong: not being a boy,
The deplorable Iphis was not your child.
Ligde expected these just efforts from you.
Not having done so, you have committed two crimes:
The first was to disobey his command,
The other to let me live even for a moment.
Alas that my crib was not used as the ferry
For my crossing over Atropos's river![18]

TÉLÉTUZE

I had foreseen this. I have always told you so,
And you have ignored my words.
My warnings did not move you.
This is the result of not having believed me.
Had you deigned to follow my advice,
You would not have given your pledge so soon.
Your heart would have snuffed its imperfect flame

18. Refers to the river Styx, which represents the passage from life to death.

And you would not be afflicted as you are now
If my prudence could have governed you but a little.
Instead, you wished only to believe in your burning passion.
Children today think they are so wise
That helpful advice offends their heart.
It is a strange thing that from their young years
They wish to shake off their parents' shackles.
In my time, nature was much better ordered;
We knew better how to manage blinded youth.
But we were not in this wretched age
When virtues no longer hold any value.
Children were good and, living in fear,
They were led by kindness rather than by force.
If you are suffering, you carry the blame for it
And do not deserve to be pitied for your fate.
You have ruined everything. What must I do about it?
This beautiful bride has discovered your disgrace;
We cannot doubt it and it will be your ruin.

IPHIS

What was hidden by day, night has uncovered.
We would really have liked to satisfy our desire
And never have I been so sad and so delighted.
Her unhappiness worried me,
But possessing her delighted me also.
And although my passion was quite useless to us,
I forgot for a while that I was a girl.

I have never received so much contentment;
I abandoned myself to pleasures.
With a kiss, I appeased my feverish love
And my soul was upon my lips.
In the sweet sensation of these pointless pleasures,
I even forgot the one to which I aspired the most.
I embraced her beautiful body whose extreme whiteness
Aroused me to make room for her within myself.
I touched; I kissed; my heart was happy.

TÉLÉTUZE

Just look at yourself and you will see as much.
No one has ever heard of a love like this.
What an impression it makes on your senses!
And what did she say, when she discovered
That a man like you is a girl when naked?

IPHIS

Alas, what could she say! She was busy
Complaining to herself that she had been deceived
And her heart told me by its secret sighs
That the goal of its desires was not being met.
I kissed her breast; I fainted upon her mouth
But she felt it no more than would a log.
And she received from me as unwelcomed
A thousand kisses, not returning a single one.
The day dawned; I watched her get up and dress,

Ashamed to have become the wife of a girl.
I did likewise and took my clothes.
Her tears fell on hers incessantly.

TÉLÉTUZE

This poor girl's state is truly pitiful,
And I suffer for her with incredible pain.
But while she was dressing,
What was the conversation?

IPHIS

We did not say a word.

TÉLÉTUZE

To my mind, that is what seems the strangest.

IPHIS

She did not say a word and I returned the favor.
We kept to silence and our eyes, sometimes,
In a mutual glance, served as our voices.
We exchanged no word, but not having had her fill,
She did by spite what I did from shame.
Ha! And how right she is! And how I regret
That she is so unhappy on account of a secret!
I will give her satisfaction by taking my own life
Unless your good counsel can lessen my resolve.
I no longer have either hope or pleasure.
I welcome death. It is my sole desire.

TÉLÉTUZE

You fool! Do you mock me? Is that the remedy
To heal the affliction that possesses you?
Is that the way to retain the support I expect from you?
You would kill me to think of it any longer.
What could I propose, whatever trouble I take?
Oh god! How little joy children give us.
Follow me quickly to the temple instead of chattering.
It is no longer time to pretend: all must be revealed.

Scene 5

Téleste, Iante, Ligde, Ergaste, Nise, Mérinte, at the temple

TÉLESTE

It is here that the heavens, so favorable to us,
Want to receive from our hearts our prayers in sacrifice.

IANTE *to herself*

Although I will utter mine quite feebly,
Their kindness will be more than repaid by my thanks.

LIGDE

How obliged we are for their supreme goodness
To have gratified us with a great favor.
The happiest of mortals does not deserve as much
And the more good they do to us, the more ungrateful people it creates.
But am I mistaken or do I see my wife
And this new husband who burns only for you?

NISE

It is them.

MÉRINTE

I thought they would come to join us,

But their devotion leads them to kneel in prayer.

ERGASTE

And not without reason. Their sad faces

Are clear testimony to what I have so often said.

I predict that you will finally admit

That those who thought I was crazy are much crazier than me.

Final Scene

Télétuze, Ligde, Téleste, Iphis, Iante, Ergaste, Nise, Mérinte, Isis

TÉLÉTUZE

Join me, Iphis, my daughter . . .

LIGDE

Her daughter?

TÉLÉTUZE *continuing*

In my prayer,

With an ardent zeal, a sincere passion.

Hope of the afflicted, our last recourse,

Goddess to whom we send our prayers each day,

If ever pity can sway your heart,

Be favorable to these hearts who pay you homage,
Who, with a fervor unknown to mortals,
Embrace your altar to implore you.
Let by some means our sorrow be allayed:
That of a girl dressed as a man, that of an afflicted mother.
All of my desires you have satisfied.
Iphis, yet unborn, felt their effect.
Your cares have protected her innocent life,
When her father ordered it to be taken.
You visited me in a dream and you did not want
The hand of a mother to advance her death.

ERGASTE

Listen.

TÉLESTE

This speech is making me doubt
And I can no longer keep patient.
What! My son-in-law is a girl?

ERGASTE

Well then, am I crazy?

MÉRINTE

How unhappy I am! Gods! Who could have guessed?

ERGASTE *to Mérinte*

I am not yours.

MÉRINTE

I would be wrong to claim you as such.
But I am truly yours; nothing can prevent it.

NISE

Gods, such perseverance!

LIGDE

O unfortunate old man!
How fate is harsh to you at the end of your days!
Alas! I recall it and I can scarce believe that I am
The hateful author of such a dark endeavor.
I urged Télétuze, on the brink of giving birth
To the precious fruit of our sacred love,
Not to endure that such a heavy burden
Weigh down our family if it was a girl.
And I ordered her, in a horrible way,
To suffocate our child if it was not a boy.
Her words have awakened in my saddened mind
The picture of a crime that I had erased from my memory.
O heavens! O merciful gods! O blood! O piety!
Are you witnesses to my brutality?

TÉLÉTUZE *to Ligde*

Your command awoke in my soul a great conflict
Between the roles of mother and of wife.
I loved the first too much to wish to betray it
And it was the second that I had to obey.

Despite my heart, however, my love for you,
Imperceptibly, was becoming the stronger
When the good goddess came to see me in a dream
And returned my impulse to my duty.
I saw her in the splendor that adorns her grace
And her great brightness dazzled me.
She said these words to me (I still remember them):
"Spare your child. I promise to assist her."
After that, I have felt more horror at the loss of her innocent life;
I became more pious and less obedient.
And hence, you may judge what I have done.

LIGDE

You made Iphis, our girl, into a boy?

TÉLÉTUZE

Indeed, Télétuze, recognizing in you a cruel father,
Was a bad wife to you and a good mother to her.
My fury needed to be stirred up somewhat more
For me to extinguish the light that I had lit.
And so, for daring to live, she was disguised.
Your unjust anger was thus entirely appeased
And your disposition clearly seemed to show
That you were only an enemy of her clothing.

LIGDE

Very well. But how has Ergaste come to know this mystery
That you have wanted to keep from me so long?

TÉLÉTUZE

His sister learned that secret from my own mouth.
And judging that her brother was quite discreet,
I also took him in my confidence
So that he could help me break up the union
That you wished to settle without knowing Iphis,
And thus strengthen our position.
He has since devoted himself to the endeavor
And has loved Iphis as his beloved
While he had loved her as a friend before.
But he spoke to her of his fire merely in hints.
The secret only left his muted lips
The day he saw an imperfect marriage take place
And saw the source of his fire taken from him.
He has only done so with my permission.

TÉLESTE

All this fine reasoning, then, is only to say
That having tricked us, you will feel no shame.
Your warnings should have been delivered more promptly.
That is not how you treat respectable people
And it is too grave an insult to impose on my daughter.
I go this instant to annul this marriage.
I will not complain when I choose again
If my daughter is duped a second time.

IPHIS

No, no! Let my death end this marriage!
Let me die before the altar where I am brought!
Destiny has not been so harsh to me
As to deprive me of the hope of the wretched.
Die Iphis, though late, and become obedient.
Satisfy your father and avenge your lover!
O beauty, whose charms a girl adores,
With a single glance, honor my death.
I have tricked these beautiful eyes whose victim I am,
So who could judge my death unjustified?
I will, with this hand, justly receive
The penalty for the sin caused by my clothing.
I do not punish myself for having loved you,
For I have not sinned since you have charmed me,
But for having deceived both you and love
With the wrongful title of genuine husband.
Let one last kiss sweeten my sorrow!
Grant this pitiful service to my desires
So that I can taste in death such a precious gift
And make my death less odious to me.
Be happy. Farewell! If this fatal moment
Deprives you of one half, keep the other well
To reward the faithfulness and loyalty
Of a lover sweeter and more perfect than me.
Since I am thus forced to give you up to others,
This dagger, my only remaining possession,

Will show you by ending my days
That Iphis has as much courage as she has love.

TÉLÉTUZE *trying to stop her*

Help!

ERGASTE *grabbing her arm*

Ah, my sweet! Do not commit this crime!
Protect dearly this heart that your beautiful eyes have taken from me!

IPHIS

Why stop me? All your efforts are in vain
And my soul can still escape your grasp.

TÉLESTE *a great noise is heard*

Where does this great noise come from? I fear a stroke of lightning,
To punish our sins, will reduce everything to ashes.
The earth will gape. With all this quaking,
The temple does not sit securely on its foundation.
The altar is wailing; the idol itself is sweating.

LIGDE

Gods! I fear less this noise than what will come of it.

THE GODDESS ISIS *appears in the air*

Iphis, your secret prayers are not powerless
And I have not forgotten the fragrance of your incense.

I wish to assist you in this passion that consumes you
And will do it out of pity rather than to keep my promise.
As for you, inhuman father, rather than punishing you,
Hear the good fortune that will come to you:
I wish to shape your family to your liking
And you will no longer be father to a girl.
Her sudden transformation will ease your doubts.
Iphis was a girl; Iphis is a man
and will not retract the pledge he has given.
He will henceforth be able to consummate his marriage.

IPHIS *metamorphosed*

Oh miracle! I am a man! A male vigor
Makes my limbs stronger, as well as my heart;
My body becomes robust in the opposite sex
And I walk with longer strides than before.
Venus, who alone occupied my gaze,
Retreats before me and makes room for Mars;
Neither my skin nor my voice remains so delicate
And my voice bursts out with a stronger tone;
The breast that I hid has become smooth
And I think that my complexion has lost its brightness.
It is done. Let us be grateful to the good goddess
Who makes me feel the result of her promise.

ERGASTE

As for me, I believe none of it.

TÉLÉTUZE

Is it true, dear Iphis,
That I am the first to call you my son?
Dear gods! If that is so, then how delighted is my soul!
How your metamorphosis will lengthen my days!
Ah! I did suspect that we would all be happy
And that the sacred Isis would hear our prayers.
All this noise was not for me a fateful omen.

TÉLESTE

Ligde, do you believe it?

LIGDE

What do you think, Téleste?

IPHIS *to Iante*

Let us comfort each other, my heart, our tears are of no use:
I was a girl before, but I am no longer one.
We will begin a life of love.
I am finally a man and you are happy.
Today, Love eases his rigors
And it is only today that marriage unites our hearts.
We must hope for the light to fade
And our second night must be our first.

IANTE

If the gods have made this change in your sex,
I must also join in your satisfaction.

LIGDE

The gods be praised if they have bestowed such grace upon me!
The slightest shadow of a doubt enters my mind again,
But although my heart doubts all these words,
I have only to believe what I have always believed.

MÉRINTE *to Ergaste*

So what then, am I to suffer this shameful insult?
For the second time, you would break your word?
Enemy of my wishes! You swore before all
That Iphis being a man, you would be my husband.

TÉLESTE

Ergaste, marry her, as you have promised,
Without giving her the leisure of being your beloved.

ERGASTE

Since Love has changed the object of my interest,
If Mérinte wants me, I am also willing to have her.

MÉRINTE

If Mérinte wants you? Joy of my life!
Alas, have no doubt that she is delighted!

NISE

We must admit that the gods are quite remarkable,
Having transformed both a mind and a body.

TÉLESTE

And thus immortals change the order of things.
Indeed, in times past they have performed other
metamorphoses;
Nothing is impossible to their divine will.
For this great miracle, let us praise their power;
Let us admire their deep wisdom
And the means that they have to govern the world.
And let us think that, in fact, we and these lovers
Receive from them the object of our satisfaction
And that if destiny was left up to chance,
They would not attempt to go against nature.

IPHIS

You must truly believe it; after all the kindness
Their generous hand has shown in fulfilling our wishes,
Admitting that we hold from them what they can take back
Is the least of the duties we owe them.
For the rest, if my excessive happiness
Leaves your hearts unconvinced,
If you do not judge my words to be truthful,
I will show you some very palpable results
And my dear half will convincingly
Prove, in nine months, that Iphis is a man.

END

About the Contributors

Marianne Legault is associate professor of French and teaches seventeenth- and eighteenth-century literature at the University of British Columbia, Okanagan. She has published on Isaac de Benserade, representations of female intimacies in early modern French literature, and seventeenth-century women's fairy tales.

Ramine Adl is associate professor of French at the University of British Columbia, Okanagan, where he teaches French language and literature. He previously collaborated with Marianne Legault in producing *Female Intimacies in Seventeenth-Century French Literature* (2012), the English translation of *Narrations déviantes: L'intimité entre femmes dans l'imaginaire français du dix-septième siècle* (2008).